In Their Own Voices

AFRICAN WOMEN WRITERS TALK
Edited by
ADEOLA JAMES
Head of the Department of English
University of Guyana

JAMES CURREY • LONDON
HEINEMANN • PORTSMOUTH (N.H.)

James Currey Ltd
54b Thornhill Square, Islington
London N1 1BE

Heinemann Kenya
Kijabe Street, PO Box 45314
Nairobi

,Heinemann Educational Books Inc
70 Court Street
Portsmouth, New Hampshire 03801

British Library Cataloguing in Publication Data

James, Adeola
In their own voices : African women writers talk.
1. English literature. African women writers, 1960–.
Critical studies
I. Title
820.9'9287

ISBN 0–85255–508–3
ISBN 0–85255–507–5 pbk

Library of Congress Cataloging-in-Publication Data

In their own voices : African women writers talk / edited by Adeola James.
p. cm.
Includes bibliographical references.
ISBN 0–435–08043–1
1. African literature (English)—Women authors—History and criticism.
2. Women and literature—Africa—History—20th century,   3. Women authors,
African—20th century—Interviews.   I. James, Adeola.
PR8340.5.15   1990
820.8'9287'096—dc20   88–77796
CIP

Typeset by
Colset Private Ltd, Singapore
in 10/11 pt Paladium
Printed by
Villiers Publications Ltd.,
26a Shepherds Hill, London N6 5AH

Dedication

Dedicated to the writers themselves;
my four daughters; my four sisters;
and all my lovely sisters all over the world:
for a revolutionized Africa and a happier tomorrow
for all our children.

Contents

Contents

Introduction

In Their Own Voices is a collection of interviews with African women writers, in which they discuss their creativity in the light of the two major, irreversible, though accidental facts of their lives – being born an African and a woman.

During the three decades that African writers have engaged in their art, criticism has developed in retrospect. How else can it be, since the dancer dances in accordance to the tune? Many writers have objected to prescriptive criticism, feeling that they write according to their inspiration and should not be asked to fulfil any real or imaginary social purpose.

However, the experience of hindsight makes it clear that writers, as cultural workers, are not apart from other workers in their society. A deep-seated desire to contribute to the debates and struggles for development that are going on in their time is what inspires their writing.

Common themes in African literature have been the devastating effect of Africa's contact with Europe, and the rehabilitation of Africa's cultural heritage to mitigate, heal or correct some of the injuries inflicted by colonialism. Some writers have addressed the conflict of the traditional world with the modern world Africa is aspiring to build; specifically, the problems of polygamy, infidelity, corruption and abuse of power, and the anomaly of human sacrifice.

The African writer's language, as the vehicle of her imagination, is shaped by her culture and at times by the fact that her mother tongue is not English. The language is often, therefore, coloured by the oral tradition, replete with proverbial sayings, information passed down from the elders, colloquial reportage, and sometimes the rambling that often characterizes our style of greeting and passing on of information.

To say that the creative contribution of African women writers has

1

Introduction

not always been recognised is to put the case mildly. In fact, the woman's voice is generally subsumed under the massive humming and bustling of her male counterpart, who has been brought up to take women for granted.

Women writers, during the twenty-five years since they started being published, have made a significant contribution, which, until recently, has been only grudgingly acknowledged. Flora Nwapa's *Efuru* was published in 1966, and Ama Ata Aidoo's *The Dilemma of a Ghost* in 1965, yet Flora Nwapa, quoting Ama Ata Aidoo, complains that, 'Some male critics don't even acknowledge female writers. Every artist thrives on controversy, so you are killing that writer if you don't even talk about her. To be ignored is worse than when you are writing trash about her'.[1]

The Decade of Women, culminating in the celebrations in Nairobi in 1985, helped to highlight the contributions and capabilities of women all over the world, resulting in a more deliberate focus on women. A spate of scholarly studies on women has emerged in answer to calls from women's movements. The significance of all this Ama Aidoo places in its proper perspective in the following words:

I don't think the Women's Movement has done anything that one would not have done. I don't think that one woke up one morning and found that they were talking about the development of women, and one should also join the bandwagon – no. What it has done is that it has actually confirmed one's belief and one's conviction. Our people say that if you take up a drum to beat and nobody joins, then you really just become a fool. These women's movements have helped in that it is like other people taking up the drum and beating along with one.[2]

It has been suggested that the situation of women is the key to a critique of society. If that is the case, what women writers have to say about their societies should receive serious attention, instead of the general disregard or head-nodding that is usually the case.

Perhaps I should say something more personal about the genesis of this work. I had outlined my project for my study-sabbatical, which was to be an autobiographical study of African women writers through interviews. At the beginning of my leave in October 1985, I attended the conference on Black Women Writers and the Diaspora in East Lansing, Michigan. The various exchanges heard at that conference convinced me that there was room for a study like the one I had in mind.

It was also there that I came across the book *Black Women Writers At Work* (US: Oldcastle, 1984), which reinforced my earlier conviction that my project was not only viable but necessary to complement what has been done for Black women writers in the United States. As was emphasised at the conference, we belong to one world. In spite of, or because of our history and distance, our destiny is inseparable. Therefore bridges need to be built across time and space. My indebtedness to the earlier book will be recognised by anyone who is familiar with it. This indebtedness is observable both in the numerous questions I pose to the writers, as well as in the general tenor of my enquiries.

A nation's development can be judged by its treatment of its women. The Scandinavian countries are recognised as being among the most socially advanced, with comparative freedom and equality for women. African society, which is still 80 per cent rural, has preserved traditional attitudes towards women. Even among the educated, who, ironically, adopt modern technological gadgets and allow their children a lot of freedom, the attitude to women remains unchanged. Most educated men look for simple and unsophisticated women as wives. 'Acada' women are uncontrollable, as Nigerian men say of graduate women. The 'acada' women, on their part, have learnt to take care of themselves. Preferring their profession to marriage, some of them use men to have children without entering into a domestic arrangement.

Such attitudes have serious implications for our development and survival. While men have traditionally been the subject of history, we are now beginning to look at women's lives as presented through their creative writing, conscious that any genre offers only a partial view of the whole. 'To understand women's life a great variety of sources must be read and approaches for commenting on them defined.'[3] One approach is that of interviewing women writers to explore what motivates their writing, what being African and a woman mean for their individual creativity, the various constraints they encounter in trying to write and how they have managed to overcome them. Questions arising from these concerns are designed to enhance our understanding and appreciation of their creative works.

The questions I ask fall broadly into two categories: the more general, or public, and the more personal. I am interested in the particular cultural constraints the writers have had to overcome as Africans and women; what they feel is the influence of the various women's movements which have grown up in recent years; how they relate with male writers; why there is no recognised female equivalent of Chinua Achebe, Wole Soyinka or Ngugi wa Thiong'o; is there an African aesthetic?

The more personal questions are intended to illuminate and clarify the individual's creative work. For example, how does the writer cope with the multi-faceted roles of parent, wife and writer? Are the roles of 'writer' and 'woman' in some ways incompatible? What is the attitude of their family to their writing? What advice would they offer to aspiring African women writers? Other points raised are the question of writing in the vernacular, the difference between the female and the male points of view in literary creation, the handling of characters, the political environment and the female artist and the problems of publishing.

In the course of the interviews, we discover that women writers have been no less concerned than men to articulate and denounce the poverty, corruption and destructive practices that have impeded development in Africa. At the same time, women writers appear to treat more intimately the themes of love and death, transcendence and the struggle to rise above the traditional limitations responsible for women's underdevelopment and oppression. Their pervasive theme can be summarised as the shared journey towards a new dawn for women and for Africa.

In formulating my questions, I have been very aware of the debates within feminist criticism. Arising from these, I ask what is the particular relationship of women writers in Africa to our traumatized civilization and societies? How close does literature come to other expressions of African women's experience? Is it the case that there is a deliberate effort to put down or ignore writings by women (many men actually boast about their ignorance of what women write!) and that women writers are often exploited mercilessly by their publishers?

The relevance of the last question is illustrated by my own personal experience. It is the story of how a manuscript that has been advertised has never been published. It was kept by a publisher, who had agreed in writing to publish for four years. The publisher then decided not to go through with it because the cost of producing it would be too high, and a recent book produced by them had not sold as well as expected.

In desperation, I sent the only copy returned to me to another publisher, anxious to convince them that it was already more or less a book. It had already been worked on and only needed a cover and good marketing. To my utter dismay, three months later I had a letter of apology from this second publisher, saying that the manuscript had been lost in the mail while it was being sent to be read! The final blow came after I had delivered the only copy I had left, by hand, to another publisher, who, months later, told me she had lost her suitcase on a transatlantic journey with my manuscript inside. I have also had the agony of seeing an article I had sent to a journal, which was never acknowledged, published with minor changes, under someone else's name. The fact that I am not alone in these experiences is underscored by the Black American writer, Toni Cade Bambara's statement that: 'There are a helluva lot of things writers need to know about markets, copyright laws, marketing, managing money, taxes, the craft itself, etc, that can more easily be mastered if people pool their resources.'[4] The politics of publishing is only one major reason for writers to get together and exchange experiences. This is especially urgent for African writers in neo-colonial societies, where publishing is dominated by the multi-nationals. Indigenous publishing houses in places like Nigeria, Tanzania, Zimbabwe and Kenya suffer from the scarcity of foreign exchange needed to import the necessary equipment, and from problems of distribution.

This anthology represents one way of coming together. What I discovered in the course of conversation was that for these writers, the intensity of their lives and commitment is lived at all levels and finally rendered to us in their works. One cannot ultimately distinguish the literary from the political and this is reflected in the interviews. This anthology is by no means all-embracing and has many obvious gaps. It is my regret that I have had to concentrate on anglophone areas of Africa because of limited finance and accessibility. Even then, Kenya and Nigeria receive the greatest exposure. The end of the Decade of Women, celebrated in Kenya in 1985, has opened up new vistas for Kenyan women and made them more communicative and conscious of their powers. It is a pity, however, that the earliest Kenyan female writer, Grace Ogot, is now so preoccupied with civic duties that she had become unavailable. However, this book can be considered the first in a series; obvious sequels would be anthologies of interviews with francophone African women writers and women writers of the Caribbean.

Even more regrettable is the fact that Bessie Head's voice, one of the most potent and compelling, was permanently silenced by her death just before I was able to reach her in Botswana. I first wrote to her about my project at the end of January 1986. Her reply was dated 23 March and received in April. In Ghana, in May, in the presence of Efua Sutherland, I learnt that Bessie Head had died suddenly the previous month. It took me some time to recover and to re-affirm my faith in the validity of the project. I must have been one of the last people she corresponded with before she succumbed to hepatitis. There was no mention of illness in her letter, only a suppressed note of disappointment and disillusionment with pseudo-scholarship and exploitation. In the absence of an interview and as a tribute to her, I offer these quotations as her voice immortalized in her works. She writes in the short story collection, *The Collector of Treasures*:

> The ancestors made so many errors and one of the most bitter-making things was that they relegated to men a superior position in the tribe, while women were regarded, in a congenital sense, as being an inferior form of human life. To this day, women still suffered from all the calamities that befall an inferior form of human life.[5]

Bessie Head's life epitomises the personal convulsions an African woman has to undergo to become a writer, to marshal her life daily, to draw from herself all her powers to fight the obstacles in the way of her becoming a harbinger and a frontierswoman for her people. Running through all the statements and conjectures by our women writers is a strong affirmation that Africans can take control of their destiny, and will not always be in a position of weakness. Bessie Head has summed this up for us beautifully in her novel *A Question of Power*. Elizabeth, at the end of her harrowing struggles, armed with her new vision, has an insight that: '. . . people's souls and their powers were like sky birds, aeroplanes, jets, boeings, fairies and butterflies; that there'd be a kind of liberation of these powers, and a new dawn and a new world.'[6]

The interviews are characterized by frankness because we have now come to the realization, more than ever before, that our world will be destroyed unless we do something urgently to save it. In the early 1960's, we denounced colonialism; today, we need to speak out, to join together across the continents to save ourselves, and to begin to prepare a viable future for our children. This is the only way we can arrest the cycle of suffering, poverty and oppression that is the lot of the majority of our people. The subjects discussed by the women in the following pages are the same problems that have faced Africa throughout the ages: slavery, colonialism, failure, post-Independence disillusionment and remedies for the future. Women have been left out of the planning, and who can say that all the failures might not have stemmed from this tragic oversight.

Our problem is that we have listened so rarely to women's voices, the noises of men having drowned us out in every sphere of life, including the arts. Yet women too are artists, and are endowed with a special sensitivity and compassion, necessary to creativity.

The purpose of this book is, therefore, to begin to change the status quo, bringing women's voices to the fore, not as a token concession, but as a moving and determining force. Reading the experiences of others recorded here, and seeing their tenacity, courage and dogged determination should encourage more women to come out through creative writing.

So I present this book in the hope that it will somehow satisfy our longing to be heard speaking in our own voices, and may help to correct the imbalance that has contributed to our underdevelopment.

Notes

1. Flora Nwapa, quoting Ama Ata Aidoo, in an interview from G. Hull (ed), *Black Women Writers at Work* (US: Oldcastle, 1984).
2. Ama Ata Aidoo: ibid.
3. G. Hull, op. cit.
4. Toni Cade Bamabara: ibid.
5. Bessie Head: *The Collector of Treasures* (UK: Heinemann, 1977), p. 92.
6. Bessie Head: *A Question of Power* (UK: Heinemann, 1974), p. 205.

Ama Ata Aidoo

Ama Ata Aidoo, author, poet, playwright and short-story writer, was born Christina Ama Aidoo in Ghana in 1942. She attended school there and was one of the first generation of graduates of the University of Ghana in Legon. She began her literary career by winning a prize in a short-story competition organized by Ibadan's Mbari Club, a famous cultural workshop of the early 1960's in Nigeria. Her published collections include two plays, *The Dilemma of a Ghost* (1965) and *Anowa* (1969); a collection of short stories, *No Sweetness Here* (1970); a novel, *Our Sister Killjoy* (1977) and a collection of poetry *Someone Talking to Sometime* (1985). She has taught English and African Literature in various African and American Universities. She is known and admired for her forthrightness and her agonizing over the fate of Africa, past, present and the future. It is this deep love that she feels for her people that informs all her writing. Ama Ata Aidoo is probably the best known African woman writer, a recognition she deserves as her art has attained the maturity worthy of her talent and dedication. Commenting on her writing, Alice Walker remarks: 'It has reaffirmed my faith in the power of the written word to reach, to teach, to empower and encourage.'[1]

Works quoted: *Our Sister Killjoy* (1977), *Anowa* (1969).

1

Ama Ata Aidoo

This interview was conducted in Harare, Zimbabwe, 13 July 1986.

Adeola: My first question is concerned with the writer's responsibility and audience. As one of the first modern African writers, you must have reflected on this important aspect of creativity. What are your views?

Ama: I have reflected on it, I don't know how often. I think that the whole question of the writer's relationship to her society has to do with language. I don't know whether you thought of it that way when you were asking me the question. But here we are, writing in a language that is not even accessible to our people and one does worry about that, you know. For instance, writing in English makes it possible for me or any African writer to communicate with other people throughout the continent who share that colonial language. On the other hand, one's relationship to one's own immediate environment is fairly non-existent or rather controversial. These are some of the ideas that one comes up with. I have not pretended to myself that I have an answer. I have thought also that, whilst one is aware of the language issue as a big issue, it is better for a writer to *write*, in English, than not to write at all.

Adeola: Well, it is definitely a very important issue. I have just come from Dar–es–Salaam where I interviewed Penina Muhando who has written eight plays in Kiswahili. Yet hardly anyone outside Tanzania knows about her. She herself says that she has never been invited to any African writers' conference. So that she feels isolated. Yet this is a person who is writing for her public, and is very highly thought of in Tanzania. I am sure that other Africans would also like to share whatever she has to say because it has relevance for all of us. Isn't this difficulty of reaching a wider audience the main argument against writing in the vernacular?

Ama: I have a little exception to the use of 'vernacular'. But, anyway, that is not the point. What you are saying is that we are caught between two imponderables. The question is, do you write in your first language – your African language – and find yourself confined as a voice, almost locked up like Penina, not even getting invited to communicate with others? Or do you write in English, French or Portuguese and perhaps be able to communicate with other people but not with your own public? I think that, like most of the issues that are so worrying, in our life time, perhaps, it will be taken along with all the other developmental issues facing Africa, and within such a context it may receive some proper attention.

Adeola: Whilst we are on the issue of language, may I just ask you quickly whether you feel that the suggestion that we should have one continental language is a good idea? Kiswahili, Hausa and Arabic have been suggested.

Ama: I think that it is an excellent idea, there is absolutely no doubt at all about it. One can envisage that when a language is chosen the question of its validity or its qualification as an African lingua franca, is going to be debated hotly. But if it can be done, I think it would be wonderful. I have always been for that really. If we can be forced to speak English because some people colonized us, or be forced to speak French, I don't see why we as a people cannot give ourselves a nice little present of a continental language. Anyway, one doesn't even know where the energy and the political will to do that sort of thing will come from. But as far as I am concerned, if anybody starts actively working on it tomorrow, I will support it.

Adeola: What has happened to the revolutionary fervour of the sixties? I remember when I first met you in Dar–es–Salaam in 1968, it was a period of revolutionary awakening. We had Walter Rodney, then Stokely Carmichael, visiting Dar–es–Salaam. However, all the high hopes we had in Africa at Independence seem to have been dashed. Many of our well-trained people now service the machinery of developed countries, whilst some of our African countries sink deeper into unviability and confusion. In this environment of failure and attrition, how do you manage to exist as a writer?

Ama: How do I manage to exist as a writer? I don't manage. What I mean is, looking at my own work, I have not written as much as I would want to, I have not operated as fully as I would like to as a writer. But then, what does one do? One has to go on. If one refuses to survive, if one refuses to 'manage', one has given in to despair. And I don't think anybody has a right to despair, because it is not possible for any one person to have all the variables to give an answer to a particular situation. So we do the best we can and move on from day to day. I don't even know whether that is the type of answer you wanted from me. But I've tried to . . . let's see. I suppose the only way I have survived is just by keeping on hoping that sooner or later we will take up our problems meaningfully. I think that, in the post-Independence mirage, the vast majority of our people have not been given the leverage to be active participants. If I may confess a real private hope, I wish there were some African, somewhere, who, one day, would help us solve our problems. Maybe it is part of my idealism and craziness, but I do think that one day we will do something about them.

Adeola: Your writing has been part of your own active involvement in creating this new Africa and you have also participated in other ways. For example, you had the unique opportunity of having been your country's Secretary for Education (under the government of Jerry Rawlings, 1983–4). How have these experiences affected your writing?

Ama: I think that my problem – if one can describe it as a problem – is that I have always tried to act out the different aspects of myself. I just go out and do things as they appeal to me. I am not out there solving problems, because you can't do it by yourself. Writing came to me naturally. I don't know where the notion of being a writer came from. All I know is that I'd always intended to be a writer, then somehow I got myself involved in university teaching. But, underlying everything, has been this concern for the African revolution. The notion that I have been a minister isn't difficult. I thought at that time the most valid thing I could do was to be the PNDC Secretary for Education, because I believe that education is the key, the key to *everything*. Whereas I do not discount the importance of my work as a writer or the possibility of doing things with my writing, I thought that out there as minister, or whatever, you have a direct access to state power, to affect things and to direct them immediately. That is why I went to be a minister. I suppose it is all trying to work out what one hopes for, but I don't want to give an impression that, you know . . . You can see that I have a difficulty in seeing myself as a prime mover – you know what I mean? You can't do that on your own, you are linked to other forces.

Adeola: Turning to a different type of question, why is it that in the field of literature as in other fields, the African woman's voice is muted, if not completely disregarded? Why do we have no woman writer to compare with an Achebe, Soyinka or Ngugi, or critic to compare with an Irele?

Ama: Well, the question of the woman writer's voice being muted has to do with the position of women in society generally. Women writers are just receiving the writer's version of the general neglect and disregard that woman in the larger society receive. I want to make that very clear. It is not unique. Now, as to the issue of where the female Achebes and so on are, you know that the assessment of a writer's work is in the hands of critics and it is the critics who put

11

people on pedestals or sweep them under the carpet, or put them in a cupboard, lock the door and throw the key away. I feel that, wittingly or unwittingly, people may be doing this to African women writers; literally locking us out, because either they don't care or they *actively hate us*. Bessie Head died of neglect. So how is she going to be an Achebe? When nobody gives recognition to her as Bessie Head, as a woman in her own right trying to write – heh! *writing* – something relevant and meaningful?

Adeola: Do you see any distinction in the way male and female African writers dramatize their themes and select significant events?

Ama: That is a question I have always been a bit nervous about. People have asked and I have heard other women writers say that because they are women, they relate to things or select their themes or treat things in a certain way. I have not actually gone into that question in relation to myself and I don't know. I think, as a woman writer, you approach issues from your position in life, in society, in history as a *woman*. Now, as to whether the result of that position is saying things that are different from how a man would say or select them, that is a question that the critics ought to answer. But then we don't even have critics who are interested in what we are doing. So the answer probably comes back to us. I hope that in operating as a woman, that doesn't mean anything silly, in the way people think women are silly, or *anything* that is effete, or sweet and feminine.

Adeola: You are, in fact, indicating the images of women as presented in men's writing. And it is only in the writings of women that we have such significant female characters as Bessie Head's Elizabeth, your own Anowa, and Sissie and so on. So that, perhaps, if we look more carefully, there are definite distinctions, because it looks as if men present women in their own image of them. How do you wish to see that?

Ama: The thing is that, if I write about strong women, it means I see them around. People have always assumed that to be feminine is to be silly and to be sweet. But I disagree. I hope that in being a woman writer, I have been faithful to the image of women as I see them around, strong women, women who are viable in their own right.

Adeola: As a long-established writer are you satisfied with the development of African literature? What about criticism, has it measured up to the creative output?

Ama: My answer to those questions is no, no, no; no to everything. No, I have not been satisfied with the development of African literature, and criticism has outstripped creative output. And you know why. To begin with, while all African writers have many constraints to deal with, African women writers have a double problem of being women and being African. Whereas criticism has become a major business, it is the going thing, and not even half the critics are Africans. Whereas African literature can be added to only by Africans, African criticism is like meat out there in the market place, with everybody dragging at it, including people who do not care for Africans or what they are writing. But they see that it is a way of making a name for themselves as critics of African literature. Do I sound grouchy? (Hearty laughter).

Adeola: In your short life span, you have at various times been a university lecturer, poet, dramatist, novelist, critic, minister for education and a mother. Can you say what is the source of such creative diversity?

Ama: What creative diversity? You know . . . well, if you think I've been creatively diverse. But without wanting to sound too self-depreciating, I sometimes wish I had made a better success of at least one or two of them instead of branching out in all these ways. I think that it is probably genetic. My father was a highly politicized individual and an artist. My mother, in her own way, is politicized. So, looking back to my parentage I think I come from a long line of fighters. See my dedication to the poem 'Someone Talking To Sometime' ('For some of the ancestors'). My grandfather was imprisoned and killed by the British, so in a way I have always been interested in the destiny of our people. It is all from the people – the environment one grew up in, the people one has met. I knew I wanted to be a writer. I became a university teacher as a result of certain people taking a *definite decision* to rope me into university teaching. So, it is how you are born, then how you develop. I don't know if these are the answers you expected from me.

Adeola: Of these various activities, which one of them has meant most to you?

Ama: What I will honestly say is that each and every one has meant a great deal, and still means a great deal to me. I have enjoyed being a university teacher. It is an utterly satisfying occupation. But to go back to my initial response, part of the reason why I have done a little of this and a little of that is that once I am doing one I am totally immersed in it. So that it meant a lot to me to be any and all of these things.

Adeola: You didn't say anything about what being a mother means to you.

Ama: Oh, being a mother! Traditionally, a woman is supposed to be nothing more valid than a mother. Sometimes one gets nervous of such total affirmation and total negation in relation to other roles that one has played. But I think that being a mother has been singularly enriching.

Adeola: Maya Angelou says, 'I try to live what I consider to be a poetic existence',[2] meaning that she takes responsibility for the air she breathes and for the space she takes up. What kind of intensity does being a writer add to your life?

Ama: What I probably would have identified is not the intensity that being a writer has added to my life, but rather an intensity of feeling that informs me as a writer. What I am saying is that I have had to admit that I am just too sensitive to our grief, to our pain as human beings, especially as Africans, to the confusions around me. I think now that perhaps that is also very dangerous, to be so hypersensitive. I don't know whether that is what Maya meant. I have found that why I write is simply because I feel too much.

Adeola: In an interview which you gave in 1967 when you had only just published *The Dilemma of a Ghost*, you enunciated your responsibility as an African writer[3]. You said: 'I cannot see myself as a writer, writing about lovers in Accra because, you see, there are so many other problems'. Since that period you have published *Anowa, Our Sister Killjoy, No Sweetness Here* and *Someone Talking to Sometime*. In what way does your conception of your responsibility as a writer inform these productions?

Ama: Well, I suppose they grow out of these concerns. Definitely *Killjoy* is a highly political work. *Someone Talking to Sometime* is no less. I attempted writing the poem 'Of Love and Commitment' a long time ago as a result of a direct decision to write a love poem. And of course it turned out to be one of my most political poems. I think that I have admitted that I am one of these writers whose writings cannot move too far from their political involvement. But I am also now in a process of reviewing a statement like the one you've just read that I made nineteen years ago. I am beginning to say that love or the workings of love is also political. Even when it is a so called a-political treatment of love, if there is a-political of anything, it is very important that one explores the nature of human relationships, including sexual relationships. So in a way, maybe, I am not really eating all of those words. I have just written a play which explores polygamy and people in love.

Adeola: The central character in all your writings is a woman, often a very strong woman. Is it a conscious decision on your part, to explore the predicament of the African woman?

Ama: No. I mean, yes and no. I have central characters that are women because I am a woman. I think that is natural. When a man wakes up in the morning, he sees a man when he looks in the mirror. So if it is natural for male writers to create male central characters, then it should be natural for me, a woman writer, to create female central characters. In that respect there has been a conscious decision. I am aware of this whole debate about wanting to write about women, but I would have written about women anyway.

Adeola: Would you agree with Molara Ogundipe–Leslie's statement, that: 'The female [African] writer should be committed in three ways: as a writer, as a woman and as a Third World person'?[4] I must hasten to say that in the same article, the critic pays tribute to you as one of the few African women writers whose commitment spans all three categories.

14

Ama: Molara is a critic and she can make the assertion, but my own addition, or rather a slight suggestion, in terms of that formula, is in connection with what we should be committed to as Third World people. I wish that at some point it would have been possible for Molara to mention 'African'. I don't deny that we belong to a larger non-northern world and the dynamics that operate in a situation like that, but find my commitment as an African, the need for me to be an African nationalist, to be a little more pressing. It seems there are things relating to our world, as African people, which are of a more throbbing nature in an immediate sense.

Adeola: In *Our Sister Killjoy* it would appear you are experimenting with a new style, a fusion of poetry and prose in a novel. Is this a particular mode that suits the kind of reality or vision you wish to portray? I often wonder whether one can appropriately call this work a novel.

Ama: Well, I wonder too. I never describe it as a novel myself. When I have been forced to describe *Killjoy*, I have said it is fiction in four episodes. As to its verse-prose style, it was almost an unconscious decision. There was no way I could have written that book in any other style. It seems that there were different tempos in terms of the prose, the narrative and what constituted the reflections of the major character. It seems to me to be the most appropriate way to have written that book. As I said earlier on, I leave the critic to say whether it is a novel or not.

Adeola: The full-title of the book is *Our Sister Killjoy or The Reflections of a Black-eyed Squint*. You must admit that this is a very unusual title. What is the full significance of this title in relation to the theme or themes of the novel?

Ama: Actually I was aware at the time of writing and even since then that I was going to write about things that people will feel uncomfortable about.

Adeola: Things people will 'squint' at?

Ama: Yes, or I'd rather they would . . . I have been aware that between what Sissie talks about and where people are there is a kind of a gap. I was seeing Sissie as a character at whom other people were looking. In fact, I don't even know why I put myself to do that, but it was not an effort. I was looking at the character, Sissie, as I thought other people would look at her and call her a 'Killjoy' and say, 'Heck, she is looking at things with a "squint" '. You know how people are always saying, 'Things are all right, don't worry'. But people like Sissie are just a Killjoy. People love to forget, people *love* not to worry, people want to take everything as a test. And the Sissies of this world are really not satisfied. I've been very much aware of how people look at the Sissies of this world. So that is why she was created. Have I explained everything?

Adeola: Yes. The next question might even give us a clearer perception of the work. I am quoting from the opening verses of *Our Sister Killjoy*: 'Things are working out/towards their dazzling conclusions/ . . . so it is neither here nor there, what ticky – tackies we have/ saddled and surrounded ourselves with,/blocked our views,/cluttered our brains'. (UK: Longman, 1977, pp. 3–5) It is a baffling work because thematically it encompasses the history of Africa, touching on the diaspora, the history of slavery, under-development, exploitation and post-Independence failure. All are seen through the squinted eyes of a modern, educated African woman. It appears to represent your total statement so far. Have you been satisfied with its reception?

Ama: No, people have failed to understand it. I am also now beginning to admit that it has aroused resentment, as I feared it might, in many, many quarters. Either the reception has been hostile or people have simply refused to acknowledge it. One or two critics have actually taken the trouble to read the book, and react very positively to it. No, I have not been satisfied.

Adeola: One part that baffles me is Sissie's experience of lesbian love in Germany with Marija. How does this fit in with the total statement of the book?

Ama: Well, if you let loose an African girl in Europe, she is bound to come across all sorts of experiences, enriching, demoralising – ah – positive, negative, etc. It was one experience that this girl, as a character, came across. Not to have written about it would have seemed to me rather dishonest.

Adeola: How long did it take you to write *Killjoy*?

Ama: Because at the time of writing it, I was teaching, mothering and doing some other things, eventually the book took about five years. Not of course, in terms of hour by hour. There were long periods when I did not write it at all.

Adeola: Another passage from *Our Sister Killjoy*, from the last section, 'the Love Letter'. You are saying: 'There goes Sissie again, forever carrying Africa's problems on her shoulders as though they have paid her to do it'. (UK: Longman, 1977, p. 118). When I read passages like this, of which there are several. I can't help identifying Sissie with her creator. Is *Our Sister Killjoy* autobiographical?

Ama: It is not autobiographical in the sense of being a faithful recording of the experiences I have been through. Sissie is a composite creation. Definitely there is a lot of me in her. Sure, some of the things she went through, I went through. But some of the characters are non-existent in my real life. So . . . my sister, this question is terrible! We write out of our experiences. So, invariably, the characters we create are bound to exist either as reflections or rejections of ourselves.

Adeola: I ask this question because it is one that many people have asked.

Ama: Tell them to ring and ask me, 'Who is Sissie's lover? Is he someone that I know?' (Hearty laughter). Yes and no, in the sense that Sissie is bound to be something of me, but really she exists in her own right. There are some parts of me that are not in her at all.

Adeola: What have been the most crucial periods of your life as a writer, critic and teacher?

Ama: Now.

Adeola: Now! Why do you say so?

Ama: Because until now, I have been involved, as you enumerated earlier, in being a university teacher, a government minister, etc. Now, I am not teaching because I have decided to confront my writing-self head on. At other times in my life, if I have not been as productive as I would have wished, I could always blame it on the fact that I was too busy teaching in the university, too busy being in government, or making a baby. Now, I have no excuses. Do you see? That is why I say this is the most crucial time because this time if I don't produce I will have no excuse.

Adeola: I suspect that there are certain questions at the centre of your creative works uniting their creative purpose. Can you tell me what these are?

Ama: Well, I don't know. These are very broad questions but I think you realise that I've been throwing things back to the critics. What I perceive to be the unity of purpose in my work may not be what is perceived to be the unity by somebody else. But I generally think that I've *always* been concerned about us, African people, what we are doing with ourselves and so on. I think that really is central to my preoccupation. As to whether this central concern, this preoccupation, has been adequately handled in my work, I don't think that I am the best person to make that assessment.

Adeola: *No Sweetness Here* and *Our Sister Killjoy* are titles which sound pessimistic, and generally, there is certain sombreness about your writing. In our situation, is there no reason for rejoicing? Are we always going to be operating at the level of struggle or could we begin to see a different horizon?

Ama: Without wanting to apologize too much for what can be perceived as pessimism, I think that my titles occur to me as part of the whole creative process including the business of writing the book. I'm sure it happens to other writers. I have felt extremely badly about *No Sweetness Here*, I'll be very honest with you. But it was something that occurred to me. In fact, recently I've been wondering whether . . . Longman are saying that they are going to reprint *No Sweetness Here* in their so called African classics series. I've been wondering whether to do away with that title because people say it is too pessimistic.

Adeola: Your writing is usually quite sad, almost bringing tears to one's eyes, as one critic has said.

17

Ama: Well, what can I say, Adeola? I work out of my perception. If one's commitment has been maturing with one, then of course, one is not going to continue to write about the tragedies of life, but to try and see, even while the tragedies are still happening, whether there are some rays of hope. You can say this about *No Sweetness Here*, but *Killjoy* doesn't end on a note of despair. I want to say that we struggle through, in spite of the almost overwhelming nature of our grief, the horrors around us, we struggle through. One keeps looking for hopeful signs and invariably one finds them; however tiny.

Adeola: All your women are very strong. Anowa, Sissie, even Eulalie, in her own way, coped with the unforeseeable. Would it be correct to say that part of your creative purpose is to take a stand for feminism, for systematically and individually encouraging and equipping our women to develop power in all realms?

Ama: I am definitely committed, in my own way, to the development of women. On the other hand I wouldn't want to go boasting that I was flag-waving. It seems to me natural that one should see women as they are operating in their lives. I've never believed that women are soft at all. I think this basic notion of women as just human beings, some weak and some strong, probably produces women like Eulalie and the others.

Adeola: You are very political but you have not as yet written a political play. Is it because you feel that something obviously political may fail to be good theatre?

Ama: Oh, I don't think so. I've already told you that apart from *The Dilemma* and *Anowa*, I have not written any other play. But I am not so sure that I agree with what you mean by 'political' because *The Dilemma* is political, and so is *Anowa*.

Adeola: I can give you an example. I think *The Trial of Dedan Kimathi*[5] is very political.

Ama: You mean taking an obviously political theme? I see. In that sense, I have not written an obviously political play. Not because I do not feel it could make good theatre but since *Anowa* I have not written any play at all for the reasons I already stated.

Adeola: Can one read sexual warfare into your writings or are the themes better defined as 'the dialectics of love – a synthesis of pleasure and pain'? Are you conscious of this dialectic at work in your writing?

Ama: I don't believe in sexual warfare and I don't believe that we are here to wage war against one another, at all. So that lovely phrase 'the dialectics of love – a synthesis of pleasure and pain' is preferable. I haven't thought of it that way, but maybe it is there.

Adeola: Do you consider yourself a shaper of human opinion?

Ama: (Laughs) I hope someone thinks I am that.

Adeola: I am quoting 'There are no soloists after all; this is group improvisation. The literature of this moment is made up of a whole lot of voices', says Toni Morrison. Which ones among the African voices are of significance to you?

Ama: You mean African writers? I think definitely someone like Chinua Achebe, because the time when his writing first appeared, I have to confess, has always been significant for me. About that time one was a student in the English Department, one had heard, 'Jane Austen is this and that', and then one was suddenly confronted with an African writer, viable, solid and so on. I knew I wanted to be a writer, but a certain amount of confidence I managed to produce came from having predecessors like Achebe. I'm not even sure whether your question is on the notion of influences and so on.

Adeola: Not influences but people who have been significant in your development.

Ama: I've always felt that Ferdinand Oyono's *Houseboy* (Heinemann, 1966) is significant writing. I think also of Ayi Kwei Armah's *The Beautyful Ones Are Not Yet Born* (Heinemann, 1969). I find myself on the one hand objecting to that book a great deal in terms of his total vision of us, but I find passages from it so solid, I am always quoting him. There are significant voices. These male African writers who have been propped up for our attention, we cannot ignore them – Soyinka, Ngugi, Achebe, Armah. Because these are the ones that have been made available to us, we cannot ignore them at all.

Adeola: Has anyone else influenced your writing?

Ama: I come from a people who told stories. When I was growing up in the village we had a man who was a good story teller. And my mother 'talks' stories and sings songs. *Anowa*, for instance, grew directly out of a story she told me although as the play has come out, she cannot even recognize the story she told. My mother is definitely a direct antecedent. Having my daughter, Kinna, has also influenced my writing. Not only in terms of having a child with you, but because when one communicates, one has to be very careful. You and I come from traditions which don't even recognize people, their intelligence or their contribution, until they start growing grey hair. So it is good to have Kinna around as a solid opinion.

Adeola: Many people believe that it is impossible to combine writing with having a successful family life. Would you say you have had to sacrifice one for the other?

Ama: Yes, but it was unconscious. I did not set out to sacrifice family life for my writing. It just happened. Those you care for, and who care for you, invariably come into collison with you as a writer. Some women writers have been lucky to find themselves in situations which are empowering. In any case, I don't think . . . However, this again is an issue which I feel very nervous answering.

Sometimes I feel that the way I have been, I would have had a lousy family life whether my energies have been channelled into writing or not. Because it also has to do with one's moods. Whatever sacrifices have been made, I want to assure you, have not been deliberate.

Adeola: If you were writing in a different society, would your development have been different?

Ama: How would I know? I suppose if one were, say, a western woman, maybe, because there are definitely more opportunities in the western world.

Adeola: But what about for an African writing in a western country?

Adeola: Without wanting to ascribe whatever failures, whatever non-development, to the fact that I have deliberately stayed in Africa, I am aware that there are more opportunities for exposure – the radio, more newspapers, more magazines, etc. One has to be honest and admit that if one were operating from England or Europe or the United States, there would have been more opportunities for one than there have been.

Adeola: What is the attitude of your family to your being a writer?

Ama: I have always been encouraged and appreciated by my family. My mother has been a tower of strength. Any time that she had fears that I was forgetting the me that is a writer, she has always reminded me. I think my daughter and other members of my family wish that I had been a little more practical or that I had put my writing to more profitable use. But I have encountered nothing but encouragement and appreciation from my family.

Adeola: What are the main problems that you have had to grapple with as a writer, technical, social or personal?

Ama: I have not been as organized as I would wished. I cannot blame my problems on anything else but me. Perhaps because of the fact that I tend to get too enthusiastic about life, I enjoy people, I tend to spend too much time being with people and just living. A fellow writer and a friend, the Kenyan, Jonathan Kariara, kept saying, 'You write so brilliantly why haven't you written more?' I said, 'Because I've been busy living'. When you are busy living, you don't write as much. My problem has been an absence of singleness of purpose vis-a-vis myself as a writer, and just being so busy living.

Adeola: Your earliest work, *The Dilemma of a Ghost*, appeals to the sentiment of historical connection between Africans in Africa and the diaspora. Why did you consider this theme significant?

Ama: Maybe it is because I come from a people from whom, for some reason, the connection with African-America or the Caribbean was a living thing, something of which we were always aware. In Nkrumah's Ghana one met African-Americans and people from the Caribbean. In my father's house we were always getting visitors from all over. I think that the whole question of how it was that so many of our people could be enslaved and sold is very very important. I've always thought that it is an area that must be probed. It probably holds one of the keys to our future.

Adeola: Toni Cade Bambara is quoted in *Black Women Writers at Work*, '. . . bridges need to be built among sisters of the African diaspora and among sisters of colour'. Can one say that it was such conviction that made you write *The Dilemma*? In which case it must be understood as a revolutionary idea, seeing that your play was published as far back as 1964.

Ama: Yes, as I have already said, as far as I am concerned, that issue is something that cannot be considered dead. It has hardly been touched. You probably noticed in *Someone Talking to Sometime*, which is divided into three parts, the middle section has to do with my experiences in the United States. Until we have actually sorted out this whole question of African people, both on the continent and in the diaspora, we may be joking, simply going round in circles.

Adeola: When did you know you were a writer?

Ama: I knew I wanted to be a writer from about when I was eighteen, but I didn't really have the confidence to describe myself as a writer possibly until after *Killjoy*.

Adeola: Is writing a way of life for you? Can you see yourself in a situation where you are not writing?

Ama: Well, I have already seen myself in that kind of situation, when I was PNDC Secretary for Education. So it is not a question of seeing myself in the future; I have already experienced such a situation once before. That lasted for eighteen months but that is really not long enough for me to say whether I would have been able to continue to live with myself, not writing. If I had remained in government, what I can probably say is that with time, I would have been able to organize my ministerial duties in such a way that even if for half an hour a day I would have written. I cannot see myself not writing. I think I now have to admit that it is either a way of life or it is high time I saw it that way.

Adeola: What impact has the women's movement had on you as an African woman writer?

Ama: The women's movement has definitely reinforced one's conviction about the need for us to push in whatever way we can for the development of women. But I don't think that one woke up one morning and found that they were talking about the development of women, and one should also join the band wagon – no. What it has done is that it has actually confirmed one's belief and one's conviction. Our people say that if you take up a drum to beat and nobody joins then you just became a fool. The women's movement has helped in that it is like other people taking up the drum and beating along with you.

Adeola: Do you think African women writers can help to resolve some of the debates concerning our underdevelopment?

Ama: Yes, but not just African women writers but African women working with other women.

Adeola: You have published plays, short stories, poetry and a novel. You have therefore experimented with all the literary forms. Which form are you happiest with? Is there any of your works that is closest to your heart?

Ama: Maybe I will answer the question you didn't ask. Probably I am unhappiest with the novel simply because it is too many words. I think that once my uncertainties with poetry as a form and its accessibility have been resolved, what I mean, if I wasn't so busy worrying about poetry not being accessible, I am very happy with poetry. But I am happiest of all with drama. Given some other circumstances I would have liked to write more plays. I have a way of deciding at different times in my life, 'now no more plays', 'now no more poems'. I do that to myself all the time. I did that after *Anowa* when I decided that there is no point writing a play and getting it published before you've seen a full production of it. I stopped writing plays deliberately because somehow I had not managed to get *Anowa* produced before it was published. I really didn't like that at all and I told myself, I would write plays again only when there was a chance of getting the play produced before publication. I had told myself not to write poetry earlier on because writing in English is already creating a barrier between oneself and one's immediate environment, and then poetry is cryptic, it is not as relaxed a form as the novel or the short story. So I said I wasn't going to write poems. But poetry, I discovered, insists sometimes on getting written, so you have *Someone Talking To Sometime*. Yes.

Adeola: I understand that you have written some children's stories. Is writing for adults different from writing for children?

Ama: One just has to be a little more careful with writing for young people. But this is a development that, frankly, I rejoice in. I have always wanted to write for children and did not have the courage to do it until I came here and because of the need simply to survive financially, I had to respond to a request to write for young people, and I've been fascinated by the discovery that I can write for children. I am too busy rejoicing in the fact to be able to talk meaningfully about it.

Adeola: Is that children's book in the market yet?

Ama: It is not just one book. The Curriculum Development Unit of the Zimbabwe Ministry of Education commissioned me to write them and they are bringing them out in booklets, so that they will be very cheaply priced and parents can afford them. One has come out so far. I am also looking for avenues of getting them published more commercially. Flora Nwapa is bringing out the stories together in one volume in Nigeria through Tana, her publishing house.

Adeola: Critics have praised your handling of language. It is natural, sensitive and gives depth to your explorations. You yourself said in 'To Be a Woman' that no one else handles the English language the way you do.[6] How do you achieve this uniqueness?

Ama: Well, I think I was being frank and boasting a bit. But what I meant, all modesty aside, is that I like the way I handle English. It has to do with my background. I haven't tried to speak the Queen's English. I've tried to always let the flavour of my African background come through in terms of the idioms and so on.

Adeola: You have expressed a certain confidence in the significance of oral tradition when you wrote:

> *I totally* disagree with people who feel that oral literature is one stage in the development of man's artistic genius. To me it's an end in itself . . . If I had my way what I would be interested in is a form of theatre where you don't only have to produce a play – where you can just sit down and relate a story . . . If I had any strong conception of what else could be done in literature, it is this. We don't always have to write for readers, we can write for *listeners*.

What has been the connection between your writing and oral literature? Do you still hold on to the utilisation of oral literature as the best thing that can happen to our literature?

Ama: I think it is a pity that people have seen the development of literature as a one-dimensional thing. It is not. I still believe that one day, when Africa comes into her own, the dynamism of orality might be something that Africa can give to the world. That is, accepting oral narration as an artistic mode. I have not been able to do anything about it myself, but I believe it.

Adeola: *Anowa* is a very moving play although quite frightening. Anowa is a woman who insists on having a voice in the decisions that affect her life. She insists on choosing her own husband, and even in marriage, she expresses her opinion on vital matters. Anowa's argument is always sound, her only offence being that she argues with her husband, which a good woman doesn't do. The logic of the play leads one to conclude that her tragedy is the result of her head-strong insistence on having a voice. However, it is significant that Kofi Ako too is consumed in the tragedy which could have been averted had he allowed Anowa to be herself. The play clearly demonstrates that it is not ordained that only men should have clear, superior moral integrity. Recognition of this point could perhaps have averted a continental calamity. How do you see this interpretation of your second play?

Ama: I think it is absolutely valid. The fact is that women have been disregarded. In other societies, in other periods, at other historical points people have managed to put women down and still operate a viable society. Quite obviously it is not the same for us now. Look at this vast continent! Look at its army of women! It is quite *ridiculous*, really, that people, especially educated African men, operate as though women were not around. That is part of the colonial inheritance, because it wasn't like that in our societies, at least not in most of them. Although, at every stage, women have not been given that headship position, our societies have not been totally oblivious of the presence and existence of women. I think it is part of that whole colonial rubbish that our men behave the way they do. I think it is about time that they woke up and we woke up and did something about it.

Adeola: A writer does not come out of a vacuum, who do you regard as your antecedents, your mentors?

Ama: I have already mentioned Chinua Achebe in that very obvious sense, I also think, especially in the sense of me being a short story writer, I come from a people who told stories. My mother 'talks' stories and sings songs. *Anowa*, for instance, directly grows out of a story she told me although as the play has come out, she cannot even recognize the story she told. My mother is definitely a direct antecedent.

Adeola: Can you describe your mood when you write?

Ama: My mood! When I know I've done a good piece of work, even a paragraph, by my own reckoning, whatever that means, I am elated.

Adeola: What about when you finish a book then?

Ama: It's wonderful. (smiles)

Adeola: The question 'why do you write?' has provoked different interesting answers from different writers. For example, the poet Sonia Sanchez, who is your friend, replies emphatically thus: 'I write because I must, I write because it keeps me going.'[8] Have you worked out for yourself the reason why you write?

Ama: Well, for me it was always just a way of being. As I said earlier, I have been aware from a long time ago that I wanted to be a writer. I did not ask myself why. I was too young then. I think now I know, as Sonia says, that I want to be a writer because I must. Why does a carpenter want to be a carpenter? If you recognize that you have a little talent that way, then you write.

Adeola: You have spoken with great feeling in 'To be a woman' about what being an African woman and a writer has meant to you. You said, 'Once in a while I catch myself wondering whether I would have found the courage to write if I had not started to write when I was too young to know what was good for me'. (p. 259) Has it been too costly? Surely the feeling that you are part of the makers of history, one of 'the voices of vision in our time' shaping the future for our children; if one understood one's activities in this light, no price could be too costly. How do you react to this?

Ama: (Laughs) How do I react? It is all well and good being told that one is part of the makers of history. But one does not wake up in the morning and say, 'Ama Ata Aidoo, look at me, I am a maker of history'. What you know and feel are the personal things, your frustrations, your experiences in terms of the general lines you are attached to. You do not see yourself in that kind of very elevated light. You are more aware of your problems – eh hen. For me, it has been costly. But I wouldn't have it otherwise. There is no way I can say I wish I had never written or that I wish I wasn't a writer. It has all been part of the taste of living.

Adeola: We must thank you for what you are doing for African womanhood. But thanking you is not enough. We must get your books into the schools and colleges for our children to read. One can say that with the exception of a few men, Africa has not been mindful of her writers, particularly the women writers. Publishers, scholars, etc. have exploited them. That a person of Bessie Head's literary stature and talent, should die in miserable circumstances is an indictment on this continent. What do you think *can* and *must* be done in a practical way to ensure that our talents have decent lives, conducive to creativity?

Ama: What to do about African writers and African women? They are part of this whole business of development. If we are not organised enough to even feed and educate our children, to see to it that our people have basic health, it is almost a luxury to ask anybody to be mindful of African women writers. They don't even know that we are around. If anybody cared for the health of the people of this continent then an awareness of writers, including women writers, and their needs, would be part and parcel of the general caring that was taking place. But given the situation as it is, it is like crying in the wilderness.

Adeola: Do you think the existence of a women writers' association would be useful?

Ama: Yes, I think that any kind of collective move is not bad. For instance, had a women writers' association existed, whether she would have resented it or not, it would have paid some attention to Bessie Head, just going to chat to a sister . . . If there were an association like that, we could network with other groups working along the same line. But writing being what it is, I don't know whether women writers are going to have the time or even the awareness to organize something like that.

Adeola: Many writers, especially African women writers, complain about the difficulty of publishing and the resultant discouragement to write. You obviously don't have this problem but how do you think this corporate or collective problem can be solved?

Ama: I'm not so sure I don't have a problem. So far I haven't had the problem of not finding someone to publish me. But then I still have problems with my publishers, for example, questions of revenues and so on. The problems might not be totally solved, but they might be somewhat addressed by an organisation. Already some women, who have the energy and singleness of purpose, have established their own publishing firms. I am thinking of Flora Nwapa, Asenath Odaga, Efua Sutherland, Buchi Emecheta.

Adeola: In 'To be a Woman' you said, 'To date, nobody, least of all women themselves, can remotely visualise a world in which the position of women has been revolutionised' (p. 258) Would it damage or undermine the ultimate struggle for a complete social, economic and political liberation of Africa if we were to focus on the oppression of African women?

Ama: It shouldn't, but I think part of the resentment which our brothers feel about any discussion on women is because they feel it diverts from the 'main issues'. On the contrary, I feel the revolutionizing of our continent hinges on the woman question. It might be the catalyst for development. But people feel very nervous about it.

Adeola: Do you have any advice for African women and young girls who would like to write?

Ama: I think that at all costs people must write. No matter what the obstacles, what the problems, we must still go on writing. Or practising any of our arts, or paying attention to any of the things we are doing, not just writers, anybody. We have to keep on going because it's only in terms of execution, in terms of working out our commitment and living fully that even on the individual level, and certainly collectively as a people, we will survive. As for the things that would stop anybody from writing, they are so many! But we shouldn't give in to the problems. In spite of the indifference of publishers and male critics, we still have to go on. Sooner or later, somebody will have to notice that we've been around.

Notes

1. Alice Walker in *The Norton Anthology of Literature by Women*, eds. Sandra M. Gilbert and Susan Gubar (NY: 1985), p. 2348.
2. Maya Angelou: Interview in G. Hull (ed), *Black Women Writers at Work* (US: Oldcastle, 1984).
3. Ama Ata Aidoo: Interview, 1977, in D. Duerden and C. Pieterse (eds), *African Writers Talking* (UK: Heinemann, 1972).
4. Molara Ogundipe-Leslie: 'The Female Writer and Her Commitment', in *Women in African Literature Today*, No. 15, eds. Eldred Durosimi Jones, Eustace Palmer and Marjorie Jones (UK: James Currey, 1987), p. 10.

5. Ngugi wa Thiong'o and Micere Githae Mugo: *The Trial of Dedan Kimathi* (UK: Heinemann, 1977).

6. Ama Ata Aidoo: 'To Be a Woman' in R. Morgan (ed), *Sisterhood is Global* (NY: Anchor Books, 1984), p. 260.

7. Ama Ata Aidoo: Ibid.

8. Sonia Sanchez: Interview in G. Hull, op. cit.

Zaynab Alkali

Zaynab Alkali, author and university teacher, was born in the 1950's in northern Nigeria, where she was also educated, graduating from Ahmadu Bello University, Zaria. She has published two novels, *The Stillborn* (1984) and *The Virtuous Woman* (1987).

Her debut in 1984 was especially welcome as she brought a northern perspective to the rich tapestry of Nigerian literary output. She was awarded the Association of Nigerian Authors' prose prize for 1985, so impressive was her first novel.

From the interview we get the impression that we can expect greater things from her in the future. We have a promising beginning in these two works, the earlier of which has been translated into several languages.

Work quoted: *The Stillborn* (1984)

2
Zaynab Alkali

This interview was conducted by correspondence.

Adeola: I have just recently read *The Stillborn*, your first novel. I commented in my diary that it is an intriguing novel by a sensitive mind. Your novel has enriched me, a Nigerian like yourself, but from the south, by recreating vividly and concretely the felt realities of village life in northern Nigeria.

As one of the few contemporary writers in English from the north, do you feel a special responsibility to be an ambassador for your culture?

Zaynab: I don't feel any special responsibility towards my own culture. Does that sound irresponsible? Frankly, what I feel is the urge to communicate certain ideas deep inside of me and if those ideas enlighten or enrich so much as a single person, then I feel a sense of achievement.

Adeola: Can you say what inspired you to write?

Zaynab: Perhaps the general attitude of the society towards the female, commonly referred to as the 'weaker sex'. I am irked by the fact that most women have been trained to see themselves as 'weak' and 'incapable' of attaining the highest peak of intellectual development.

Adeola: Many black women writers and critics have complained that black women have received cruel treatment in our literature. Only when the author is a black woman does she have a chance. Do you agree with this view?

Zaynab: When you say 'black women in our literature' I assume you mean 'African women in African literature'. If this is the case, then I can confidently say that in African literature women are not even adequately presented, not to talk of being treated one way or another. With very few exceptions women are generally ignored and at best given minor characterization to give the story life-likeness. I am certain *some* male writers would have done away with women characters if they could.

Adeola: Are you therefore conscious of preserving a certain image of the African woman in your writing? *The Stillborn* presents heroic women – Li, Awa, and Faku. Li, 'the man of the house', is the spokeswoman for them all. When commenting on Faku's situation she says: 'Like all of us, Faku has her problems and is struggling the best way she can to survive. The method she chose should not concern anybody else'. At the end she firmly comments or rather instructs: 'We are all lame . . . But this is no time to crawl. It is time to learn to walk again'. Can you say something about the creation of Li?

Zaynab: As to the first question, preserving a certain image of the African woman in my writing comes naturally (unconsciously).

As to the second question, when I was creating Li, I thought she would come out a typical ordinary northern Nigerian woman who has to grapple with the strange ailment called culture conflict. I never imagined Li would emerge with special strengths, as I am constantly told even by my strongest critics.

Adeola: The grandmother is such a virago! I'd like to quote this vivid passage which describes her energy, one that I find unique in African literature. It is grandmother's tirade to the villagers:

> 'Men of this village . . . listen to my words. I was married fourteen times in the eastern part of this land. I left for this part because I could find no lion among them. The village was filled with red monkeys, black monkeys, jungle pigs, wild cats, toothless dogs and lame cocks. Did I know, gods of my father, that I was coming to meet a worse pack? This village is full of lizards, snakes, worms and by the gods of my ancestors, cold slippery fish'. She bellowed with laughter. 'And the women? A pack of domestic donkeys with no shame. When they are not under the whip of their wizard husbands, they are busy plotting witchcraft'. (p. 53)

This is a powerful passage, and a powerful creation too. Can you tell me the impulse behind this creation?

Zaynab: The impulse behind this creation? Well, I am a good listener, I listen to people even when I do not appear to be doing so. Although I left the village at the age of ten, I still remember, vividly, being in the company of old women who liked to castigate the new breed of young men who 'sacrifice their manhood at the altar of civilization'.

Adeola: Li is so unique that she defies comparison. Yet I am tempted to compare her with such great creations as Ama Ata Aidoo's Anowa, Penda in Sembene's *God's Bits of Wood*, and Rebeka Njau's Selina in *Ripples in the Pool*. Who are your antecedents?

Zaynab: Literary antecedents? No one that I am conscious of, but there are certain writers I greatly admire, such as Chinua Achebe, Ngugi wa Thiong'o, Elechi Amadi, Okot p'Bitek, Sheikh Hamidou Kane and among the young breed, Odia Ofeimun, Isipdore Okpewho and Niyi Osundare. I also admire western writers like Thomas Hardy, Catherine Cookson and Ernest Hemingway. It is possible that I could have been influenced one way or another by them.

Adeola: How do you find writing in English, since your first language is Hausa, with its roots in Arabic and Bantu languages? Would you not feel more comfortable writing in Hausa? Have you considered this and the implications it might have in terms of your readership?

Zaynab: I find writing in English agonizing, to say the least, especially when it comes to dialogue. My characters in 'real life' do not speak in English, and in the act of translation, the native idiom is completely lost, as are the meanings of certain expressions. Naturally, I would feel more comfortable writing in my own language but the audience, as you know, would be limited. Maybe translation could help, I have considered that too.

Adeola: What impact has the women's movement had on African women writers?

Zaynab: Not much. In my view, the movement interferes with women's writing. People tend to look at most literary works written by African women as 'feminist literature'.

Adeola: You are a mother and a university teacher. What obstacles have you had to struggle against in order to become a writer?

Zaynab: Time. I wish there were more hours in a day.

Adeola: It is often said that writing is a lonely art and it is very rare for a woman to combine a successful family life with being a writer. How have you found this?

Zaynab: Writing hardly interfers with my family life. I am married to a man who works around the clock as Vice Chancellor of a university and I would be lonely if I were not busy. The children were born into this very busy family, as a result of which I already have two writers in the making, a fifteen year old novelist and a thirteen year old playwright.

Adeola: How do you fit writing into your life?

Zaynab: Snugly.

Adeola: Does your writing follow a definite pattern of commitment or are you telling stories that happen to be in your head?

Zaynab: I have no stories in my head. I write as I feel inspired by the happenings around me. So the physical, psychological and moral set-up of my society determines what I write about. I would not know if my writings follow a definite pattern or commitment until I have written several.

Adeola: The title of your second novel, *The Virtuous Woman*, sounds highly moralistic. Can you comment on that?

Zaynab: *The Virtuous Woman* is a novel written especially for adolescents. It is deliberately moralistic, written in the spirit of the W.A.I.* campaign. I feel our children are in desperate need of morals, so I created some character models.

Adeola: Tell me about the response to your novels? Are you satisfied with it? Do you know how widely read they are?

Zaynab: The response is simply *fantastic!* Since 1984, I have collected about 25 literary reviews and criticisms inside and outside the country, in journals, magazines and newspapers. *The Stillborn*, as far as I know, is being read in Europe and America. Part of it was recently translated into German.

Adeola: What is the response of your family to your being a writer?

Zaynab: Natural. I come from an artistic family. My mother sings. My maternal grandmother was a composer/singer and my maternal grandfather was a drummer. There was an old joke that my grandparents married in the village dancing area.

Adeola: Like most African writers your novels are suffused with the traditional wisdom of our foreparents, in the form of proverbs and other traditional speech patterns. How do you incorporate oral traditions into your writings? Have you made a special study of oral traditions or do they occur to you naturally?

Zaynab: When I was a child, oral traditions used to be part of our growing up. I was born in the 1950's. Grandmother told stories to age-groups from around 7.00 to 10.00 p.m. Ordinary conversations were punctuated by local proverbs and traditional mannerisms. Even today, daily conversations among the older generation still retain some of the traditional speech patterns. Unfortunately, the new generation no longer has any need for the traditions. The truth is, they hardly speak the native language. Remember, they go to nursery at 3 years! and then there's television and video between the blessed hours of 7 and 10 p.m.

Adeola: Achebe has said: 'An impressive number of the major contemporary African writers have been unanimous in declaring their writing in the service of their people's culture. . . .'[1] How do you see your role as an African writer and a woman?

Zaynab: I see my writing in the service of humanity, with special reference to Africa and the Third World. I strongly believe that whatever the theme, whatever the culture, basic human experience is the same. I may be biased, though, towards the general condition of women in the modern world.

Note

1. Chinua Achebe: 'The Uses of African Literature', in *Okike* 15, August 1979.

* War Against Indiscipline was a campaign launched by the Buhari regime, which toppled the civilian government of President Shagari in Nigeria in 1983.

Buchi Emecheta

Born in 1944 in Lagos to parents from eastern Nigeria, Buchi Emecheta received her education in Lagos up to secondary level and later studied Sociology at the University of London.

She was perhaps the first African writer to address the issue of feminism overtly. All her writings benefit from her sociological training in that they focus attention on sociological issues such as black oppression in a white society, man-woman relationships in traditional society, and tradition versus modernity. Along with other stalwarts like Ama Ata Aidoo, Bessie Head and Flora Nwapa, Emecheta has helped redress the somewhat one–sided picture of African woman that has been delineated by male writers. Her contribution includes *In the Ditch* (1972), *Second-Class Citizen* (1974), *The Bride Price* (1976), *The Slave Girl* (1977), *The Joys of Motherhood* (1979), *Destination Biafra* (1981), *Naira Power* (1981), *Double Yoke* (1981) and *The Rape of Shavi* (1986), and an autobiography, *Head Above Water*.

3

Buchi Emecheta

This interview was conducted in London on 21 August 1986.

Adeola: In spite of more than two decades of Independence in Africa, we are still very much a people without direction. We are despised and not taken account of. To what extent do these realities affect your work?

Buchi: It means sometimes you feel a sense of inferiority, especially some of us African artists living abroad. Sometimes you feel you want to identify yourself as an African writer, then you see Africans being humble and you ask, 'Am I not cheating myself wanting to identify myself as an African writer?' You find all the time you are faced with this dilemma.

Adeola: With you living here in England how do your children identify themselves? And for whom do you write seeing that you are based here, in a non-African country?

Buchi: The children were born here to African parents. The best I can do, then, is to see that we go to Africa regularly and see what Nigeria is like. What is surprising is that none of them wants to work there.

Adeola: Why is that?

Buchi: It is because they notice the apathy and slowness about every-thing. Last night my first son was telling the other one who I am taking home, 'You will like the weather. But the people, you will see through them in three hours'. This is because their attitude to life is different from ours.

Adeola: They are free from the kind of emotional attachment that you and I feel towards our country. It is that attachment that makes you set your novels in Nigeria because you wish to see a change. Do you think this change will take place in our life time?

Buchi: Well, as I am beginning to say in some of my later novels, half of

35

the problem rests with the women. They are so busy bitching about one another, the men say the women are acting just as is expected. But when you deal with foreign women, say you go to a place like Norway, or even here in England, all you have to do is give a talk and they appreciate you and express solidarity with you. But it isn't so in our own country. The usual reaction is, 'So she has written a book? I know who did it for her'. This type of cynicism is still there, especially among the educated class.

Adeola: You are not the only writer who has mentioned this. In East Africa several women writers complained about their own friends saying that it is their husbands who wrote their books for them. And you feel that the actual development rests in the hands of women?

Buchi: I think it does. If we as women don't put one another down, things should work out better. Look at western society; for instance, some English women tied themselves to poles at the turn of the century before they could have a vote. But if you say something like that at home, they will reply, 'It is not done, our people don't do it'. That means you can't change it. For example, take the case of when a woman loses her husband, she is supposed to mourn for nine months, like a crazy woman she won't have a bath for nine months. When anybody suggests changing that, our women don't like it. Women who have gone through it insist that their daughters-in-law mourn for nine months as they have done.

Adeola: The majority of Nigerian women writers are Igbos. Why is this?

Buchi: The Yoruba language is good for dramatists. If you look at it, our own language, the Ibo language, is like German, it is very ironic. If you look at the Yoruba language, the rhythm and the sound and everything are richer than ours. Culturally, especially in the visual arts, I think the Yoruba have it. But people don't look at that. Because that is what pushed Wole (Soyinka) up, not so much his novels but his drama – the singing, the drumming, the traditional rhythmic music and so on. For instance, when burying the dead the Yoruba will be singing most of the time, but our people will start a story which will go on until the person is buried. Our people have this way of prolonging things. The last time I went home I witnessed a burial. The story telling goes on for a longer period now, since the dead can be placed in the mortuary almost indefinitely, until they gather everything together for those elaborate and wasteful burials that our people indulge in. The women will start singing the story today where they left off the previous day. If they are tired, they will introduce a fable, which is what Chinua Achebe is noted for.

Adeola: I have an Igbo brother-in-law and I was discussing with him why it is that the Igbo culture has produced almost all our female

male writers like Chinua Achebe, Elechi Amadi, ~~~nsi and so on. He thinks that it is because of the ~~ ~ne Igbo society, and those cultural practices, for example the *Osu*. Such cultural practices allow the writers to explore and discover profound, imponderable themes for their writings.

Buchi: When we look at the *Osu*, the Yoruba have story-tellers too. Take also your Yoruba naming ceremonies, they are much more visual.

Adeola: Maybe some Yoruba women have to sit down and do some writing.

Buchi: Yes. It is necessary.

Adeola: Can you tell me what in your personal life and background is responsible for your becoming a writer?

Buchi: Mine was because I didn't go to my own village as a young person. I went after I finished my education. I was intrigued by the whole way of life. For example, some women will sit for hours just peeling egusi (melon seed) or tying the edge of cloth or plaiting hair. Some will be telling stories, and not to young children. I saw it and I used to sit with them. I liked the power these women commanded as story-tellers. Since then, I thought I would like to be a story-teller myself. But, unfortunately, I can't write stories in my own language. I can write Yoruba but not Igbo, so I have to write in English. On top of that, we marry very early in my own area, so by the time I was twenty-two I already had five children and the marriage had broken up. I had come to this country with my husband, so I decided to go to university here. In my first year, during the holiday, I couldn't work because my oldest child was then five years old and I had four others. So the only thing I could do was to write. That was when I started writing. After several years of failure and rejections my work was accepted for publication. So my first book was published in 1972, when I was still a second year undergraduate.

Adeola: Nobody would suspect you experienced this problem of rejection.

Buchi: Ah! with my first book, *In The Ditch*, I felt I had enough rejections to fill the world.

Adeola: How did you manage to get over that?

Buchi: I think that is where my Igboness came in. I think the Igbos are very stubborn. If I want to drink from this cup and someone says, 'no', I just have to do it. It is that or nothing. I will keep on trying. The whole of 1971, and in fact, 1970, almost every day I kept sending manuscripts to different publishers. Religiously every Friday they came back with comments like 'good but this and that'. Eventually they started publishing them.

Adeola: Is it because you persisted that you succeeded?

Buchi: Exactly; when you've written the first one if it is one thing you want to do, and you persist, before you realise it, you get there.

Some young people come to me and ask, 'How much do you get?' I tell them, 'You don't think about the money when you are first starting'. I'm afraid that is one of the reasons why a lot of Nigerian women, in particular, are not interested in writing. We are so money-oriented, wherever you go people judge you by what you wear. You can't tell your friends, 'I can't do it for the next three years because I am writing a book'. They will laugh at you. Furthermore, writing is not one of those professions where people give you something to start on, you just continue to struggle on your own. And the moment you entertain doubts in your mind, you are going to fail and when the book is rejected, you are going to be very discouraged. It is easier when there is money in the family. For instance, my son left Cambridge three years ago and is trying to be a writer. He has not earned a penny. It is only now that he is making some headway. At home, people would be unsympathetic and tell him to go and earn some money.

Adeola: You can't blame him, he is trying to follow in your footsteps.

Buchi: Yes, I try to push all my children to read science, even the girls – all of them.

Adeola: Is it because earning a living by writing is a precarious life?

Buchi: Yes, and they haven't got that tenacity which I have. But it looks as if they are more interested in writing, even when they finish their science degree they still prefer to write. For example, one of my daughters is now editing for a publishing house. In fact, she edited my last book.

Adeola: So writing is a family profession now?

Buchi: It looks like that.

Adeola: How do male writers regard you?

Buchi: They pretend you are not a threat, but they feel threatened. They don't say it, but I know. They feel comfortable with other female writers who they know are never a threat, like Flora (Nwapa), who won't come out and say what she feels. I don't blame her because she lives in Nigeria, and she is a good woman. She is creating her own life, her own career, in a polygamous environment, and she keeps cool. People say she could not have written *Efuru* and *Idu*. But she wrote them and could write such books again if she makes up her mind.

Adeola: Yes, she has talent and she is a pioneer.

Buchi: Certainly, she has it in her. But it is when they see women who they know they cannot underrate, they have nothing good to say.

Adeola: Do you think living in England has made a difference to you as a writer?

Buchi: Yes, it has. I am much more forthright. I cannot afford to pretend. In Nigeria woman are riddled with hypocrisy, you learn to say what you don't feel. You learn not to laugh or not to laugh too loudly. I find I don't fit in there any more. If something annoys me, the next day you'll see it in the papers. That got me into trouble several times at the University of Calabar, where I was writer in residence in 1983. When I got fed up I stopped writing in the Nigerian newspaper, *Daily Times*, and wrote in *West Africa*, a magazine published in London. That made me even more unpopular, so much so that at one time President Shagari himself replied. I think this society gives you that freedom of outlook. Don't forget, also, that my vehicle is the English language and staying in this society, working in it, you master the nuances. Writing coming from Nigeria, from Africa (I know this because my son does the criticism) sounds quite stilted. After reading the first page you tell yourself you are plodding. But when you are reading the same thing written by an English person or somebody who lives here you find you are enjoying yourself because the language is so academic, so perfect. Even if you remove the cover you can always say who is an African writer. But with some of my books you can't tell that easily any more because, I think, using the language every day and staying in the culture my Africanness is, in a way, being diluted. My paperback publisher, Collins, has now stopped putting my books in the African section.

Adeola: I see.

Buchi: Yes, they just put them in the main shelf. They feel that my last one, *The Rape of Shavi* could have been written by anybody.

Adeola: Now what about the question of audience: for whom do you write?

Buchi: I write for anybody who can read. I've got my work translated into fourteen languages.

Adeola: Are you satisfied with the amount of literary creativity in Africa?

Buchi: Oh, no. Not at all. In Nigeria alone our population is one hundred million but how many writers do we have? In England here, look in the Sunday papers and you see how many books are being published, in different sections, and people read them. But in our own case, our men boast, 'I have no time for fiction', and want you to applaud them, not knowing that they are displaying their own ignorance.

Adeola: So, you are saying that we must read more.

Buchi: Yes, we have to read more. And then diversify what we write about. Everything coming out of Africa, in literature, is still concerned with colonialism, what the Englishman has done to us. We forget that some of us have been independent for more than two decades. It is about time we started writing about ourselves now.

Adeola: Can you describe your creative process? You seem to have a certain amount of aggression and to work twenty-four hours a day.

Buchi: No, I don't. I used to write for four hours every day except for Sundays and Saturdays. But now, I don't. My books are all being published, and they are also being sold, so I do more travelling now than writing. But I try to do at least a book a year, or one in two years. It is not aggression, it is the situations that present themselves. For instance, when I went to Calabar, in that terribly uncomfortable heat, we were expected to wear academic gowns. I'm sure the temperature was over 100°C, and it was also humid and I had just come from England. This idea of wearing academic gowns, which were designed for people in Cambridge when there was no central heating, was so ridiculous. All of a sudden, I got so angry. I saw our men, not just in academic gowns but in three-piece suits with a tie – ridiculous American type! I just threw off my own gown and the following day I wrote about it. To make matters worse, the Chancellor, one man from the north, refused to join the procession and drove his Mercedes right inside the Convocation hall, where the ceremony was taking place. In fact, they almost carried him in. When I graduated in 1974 the Queen Mother was the Chancellor of London University. She was then in her late seventies, but she stood there for four hours shaking everybody's hand, greeting us and smiling. I compared that situation with that obtaining in Calabar, where this man from Maiduguri rode into the convocation in his Mercedes, and I wrote about it. Of course, they didn't like it. I told those who objected that perhaps the man should have ridden on his horse so that we will know he is a chief. Lots of people replied, saying that I did not know my culture. That didn't bother me.

Adeola: I suppose your culture is riding in Mercedes Benz?

Buchi: Don't mind them. The next year some of the students refused to wear academic gowns. They made a smart costume which looked very nice.

Adeola: You see! People like you are needed in our society.

Buchi: But the trouble it cost me, I cannot recount it. I knew they wouldn't publish it in Nigeria, so it was published in *West Africa*.

Adeola: This leads me to the question of commitment. Molara Ogundipe–Leslie, a Nigerian critic, wrote that an African woman writer should be committed in three ways: as a woman, as a writer and as a Third World person. What do you think about this statement?

Buchi: What does she mean by commitment as a woman? A writer is a writer, and writing is sexless. But you can write from a particular situation, for example, if you are a working class person and you want to highlight the oppressed conditions of your class, or you want to write about women and men. I suppose they are all connected. But the financial question is still a determining factor in being a writer. You mentioned the Nigerian writer, Ifeoma Okoye. It took her six months to write a novel for which she was given an advance of 1200 naira.

Adeola: (alarmed) She can't live on that.

Buchi: How can she live on that? It is a good thing she has a husband. So you cannot ask a woman like that to be committed. She can only write spasmodically. She is probably still teaching, looking after the family and being a good wife. But here in England, one can live off writing alone. People read a lot. So, after the first two or three books are published you can afford to live off writing.

Adeola: But not all African writers can afford to live in England.

Buchi: I am not talking about writers living in England alone. In Africa where the population is even larger, why are writers not patronized? For instance, a good writer in Nigeria who has published two books, if they are being read, should be able to live off the books. But they are not being patronized enough. Nigerians prefer to read Hadley Chase or any other cheap American writer. So it is nice to write out of commitment. I like to be committed, we all like to be committed, but I can't stay here and judge my fellow writers in Africa, because perhaps the society doesn't allow them this kind of commitment you are talking about. Look at Bessie Head. She could have suffered tremendously because her publishers were in Europe whilst she was in Africa, and her money had to be sent down from Europe. Whereas, I could just pop into their office and tell them, 'O.K. if you don't give me my money, now, I won't give you my next manuscript', and that will make them think.

Adeola: The thing is that you are more aware of your rights vis-a-vis your publishers because you live in England. Is there not a need for writers as a group to make the publishers treat them fairly? What happened to Bessie Head is scandalous.

Buchi: Oh, yes. And it is still happening to other writers. Look at Ama Ata Aidoo, one of the very first women writers in Africa. If she were in Europe she would not have any financial problem at all.

Adeola: I feel that perhaps if there were an association of African women writers, they could discuss these matters so as to prevent their individual exploitation.

Buchi: If you notice, it is only recently that they have started inviting African women writers to conferences. It was a single-handed battle on my part. After some time, I felt so choked up, I had no time for anything else, so I told them, 'Look, there are other African women writers'. I am now also getting interested in Caribbean writers.

Adeola: In fact, something is being set up at the University of Ibadan's Institute of African Studies which will bring together African women writers and the black writers of the diaspora.

Buchi: That would be very good because women writers all over the world have their various organisations, it is only in Africa that we have none.

Adeola: You are a very prolific writer. You have published sixteen novels since you started writing, in 1972, which is a period of only fourteen years.

Buchi: Don't forget that for the past six or seven years, I haven't done anything else. I just write full time. But what I do is travel a lot and I am going to start cutting this down as well, because you cannot write as much if you have other full-time commitments. For instance, the whole academic year that I spent in Calabar, I couldn't do anything else, I just wrote some articles. Yet, I had that book, *Double Yoke* in my head all the time. It was after I had spent three months and I had nothing to show for it that I decided – this will not do at all – I preferred to leave the academic den and return to London, to my literary den.

Adeola: It has been said that writing is a lonely art. How do you reconcile that with being an African? As you know, we like to have our people around us.

Buchi: Oh, it is terrible! Not only that, when you live alone and you are writing, when you go out you tend to lord it over people. You are so impatient and you can't suffer fools gladly. But my children help to keep me sane.

Adeola: What are the questions at the centre of your creative works?

Buchi: First of all, I try to ask: why are women as they are? Why are they so pathetic? When you hear about traditional women who were very strong, you wonder, why are we today so pathetic, so hypocritical?

Adeola: Do you see any difference between the ways in which African male and female writers handle theme, character and situation?

Buchi: The difference is not only in the language, but also in the fact that female writers handle female characters more sympathetically than men. The good woman, in Achebe's portrayal, is the one who kneels down and drinks the dregs after her husband. In *The Arrow of God*, when the husband is beating his wife, the other women stand around saying, 'It's enough, it's enough'. In his view that kind of subordinate woman is the good woman.

Adeola: People are beginning to say that the real reason for the tragic disruption of society depicted in *Things Fall Apart* is because the female principle is neglected whilst the male principle, with its strong-headedness and inflexibility, is promoted above all else.

Buchi: I discussed that idea in my latest book, *The Rape of Shavi*, which is about the rape of a culture. At the end of that rape we find it is women who bring things together. Whereas, if they had allowed women to take part all along, maybe the rape would not have taken place. How many women do we have in parliament? In Sweden, a country with eight million people: forty percent of their parliamentarians are women.

Adeola: How have your creative interests evolved? You said you started by looking at the position of African women in society. Now, you are turning your attention to black women in English society.

Buchi: Yes, I have stayed a long time here and the literature of the second generation blacks is now beginning to emerge. We are beginning to become a real force. I think we need books for schools and for our own enjoyment which should be of interest to all of us.

Adeola: Can you describe your creative process? How do you conceive an idea, and how does that idea become a book?

Buchi: My first discipline is sociology. In sociology we learn about a lot of concepts. My books are based on various concepts. For example, *Second Class Citizen* is based on the clash of two cultures, *Joys of Motherhood* deals with population control and *The Slave Girl*, the tradition of slavery. I explore the concept first of all, like in *Joys of Motherhood*, where I created a woman who had eight children and still died by the wayside. So what I do is to get the concept clear, then look for the setting. Most of my books have been set in Africa. Now I am doing a book called *Gwendoline*, on the Caribbean immigrants who came to England and how their culture was destroyed.

Adeola: Well, that leads me to the next question, what barriers, both inward and outward, do you face in attempting to produce literature?

Buchi: I have answered that question partly. There is another barrier also, the barrier of language. When one first came here one discovered that the English we studied at home was the classics – Shakespeare, Jane Austen – and that people here don't use that language. English is not my first language, yet as a writer you are competing with other English writers. For example, one publisher wrote to me and said he will publish my book if I can change my name to Edith Smith or something like that. But I didn't give in.

Adeola: What impact has the women's movement had on African women writers?

Buchi: It has had a great impact. When I first started writing feminist novels, that is, novels about women's issues, I thought I was going to be alone. But when I went to Nigeria I found there were other writers. It has helped also in bringing our women out of Africa. For example, the feminist movement in England brought Flora Nwapa and Ama Ata Aidoo here recently. At the various conferences they always make sure that black women are well represented.

Unfortunately, there is still a hierarchy among women. For example the very white ones, feel they are the big guns in the movement. But it is helping our women in that it is giving them confidence.

Adeola: I am interested in looking at generations. How would you compare our generation with that of our mothers? In relation to the future of our daughters, do you perceive a kind of development or is it the proverbial one step forward and two backwards?

Buchi: I think our mothers suffered more because they embraced

Christianity. The people who had it well were our grandmothers, because they had no Christianity.

Take Flora Nwapa's grandmother, for example, who was a farmer and had the courage to speak out in society. Because she wanted improvement, she sent her daughter to a mission school, where we enchain one another. Then that daughter married a man with the idea of one man one wife. When they had to go to Lagos and Port Harcourt to work, she became more of a slave, because she gave everything to the man. She had to be there to cook, to be the 'Mrs', to make sure he had a nice pair of slippers on and so on. But our own generation is now rejecting that slowly and our daughters even more. For instance, when it comes to sexual relationships, they are much more liberal than we are and that gives them a better opportunity to study the man they think they are going to share their life with. This we didn't have because we just went into marriage blindfold, trusting to luck and to God. There are many more choices now for our daughters. It is nothing bad, at least, for black girls who grow up here not to have children, or to have children when they want to have children. The African girls here make sure they have a university education before they get married. So, on the whole, they have much more freedom than we had. However, in Nigeria I am not so sure, because a woman who has children without a husband is still not respected. Whether she is a Ph.D. or not, they still talk about her. Unless she accepts the protection of any 'foolish' man so she can be a 'Mrs' somebody, she has no significance.

Adeola: How would you comment on the statement that writing is keeping track of one's own being? Would you say, from your own experience as a woman, that it is more difficult for us as women to keep track of our lives? That is, to step aside and reflect, because we are entrusted with the care of the home, the upbringing of the children and so on?

Buchi: I do agree that writing is keeping track of one's own being, especially in my own case. My first book is about my life, my mother's generation and so on. But it is also true that it is very difficult for us to keep track. The problem is finding the time to put things down. A lot of women remember everything in their head, but they have no time to really sit down and write. When I wrote *The Slave Girl*, I had never been to Onitsha, it was my mother's story. Every day, whenever she asked me to do something and I made a mistake, she would start, 'When I was in Onitsha', and she would go on and on and on, and you heard that 20 million times! You know how our mothers used to go on recalling their own lives when we went out of step? I suppose this is our oral tradition. It was from all that information that I was able to reconstruct her life.

Adeola: In order to be a writer you have to have very few distractions, and be very disciplined.

Buchi: Yes. In fact, I discussed this in *Second Class Citizen*. The first book I wrote, my husband burnt, and then I found I couldn't write with him around. Again another thing is that if I am writing and someone comes to tell me something disheartening it can upset me for days. I am what the Yoruba call *eniti o l'okan* (literally: someone without a strong heart, meaning not tough enough). My husband knew this and was very good at upsetting me. Each time he knew I was involved in writing he would say something that would cripple me mentally for days. So I decided I couldn't get anywhere with a person like that.

As the children grew older and went to university, as long as I heard from them my writing moved on quite well. But when I don't hear from them, I suddenly stop, I'll be worried until I hear from them again.

Adeola: To have survived at all as a professional woman in our male-oriented society is commendable. But you have not just survived, you are admirably truimphant. You have fought against many barriers. Even the spirits, to quote Zulu Sofola, have a way of vanishing before you. (Buchi laughs). What is the source of this energy and inspiration?

Buchi: Despite everthing I am very religious. I don't mean the Halleluiahs. Sometimes I don't go to church for a month. But basically I am one of those people who still believe in the power of prayer and prayer means suggesting to yourself what you want to do. I think this has helped me a lot spiritually because whenever I am going to do a chapter I commit it to God. I say 'God, this idea has come to me, help me to treat it responsibly'. I do this because people will quote what you have written in a book, so it is a tremendous responsibility. You recognize your gift and ask God to help you to use it responsibly. Again, I don't plan for ten years, I just take a day at a time. I say to myself, I am going to do this today. After I have done it, I am free.

Adeola: That information is very interesting and valuable. Now my last question – what advice would you give to young African women who would like to write?

Buchi: (laughs). You have to be determined. The first person you need to convince is yourself. If it is something within you, your own truth will come out. Your truth may not be my truth. If I am speaking my own truth the way I see it, I must be prepared to defend it. That means having that belief in yourself and being prepared to write it as you see it, then, eh hen. So I think the greatest person to conquer is oneself. Once you have accepted the discipline of being without money for some time, then once you have written a book, once one title is already in the market, you are all right.

Pamela Kola

Pamela Kola is Kenyan. She was educated in Kenya and later pursued a Diploma in Education at the University of Leeds. She is a teacher by profession and at present heads a nursery school in Nairobi. Her love of traditional folk-tales meshes with her profession as a nursery school teacher. Since 1968, she has been publishing folk-tales in a series known as the *East Africa When, How* and *Why Stories*. These stories preserve the simplicity and effectiveness of oral narratives.

4
Pamela Kola

This interview was conducted with Pamela Kola at the Nairobi nursery school which she heads on 25 June 1986.

Adeola: I am familiar with only one of your books, *The East African How Stories*. I enjoyed reading it because I like the oral traditions. I gather you have written several other books. Can you tell me about them?

Pamela: Yes, I have written not only *The East African How Stories* but also the *When* and *Why* stories, which have all been published. I used to be very much interested in writing but the publishing houses just let one down.

Adeola: Your experience is not unlike that of other women writers. Many complain about frustrating experiences with publishers.

Pamela: I published *The Cunny Tortoise and Other Stories* in 1980. Since then other manuscripts have been with publishers.

Adeola: All your publications seem to be on the oral traditions.

Pamela: Yes, they are. The publishing houses wanted materials for secondary and primary schools. I feel, however, that anybody can read these books because they are stories passed down by our ancestors. I heard them from my father and mother.

Adeola: Usually it is the grandparents who tell stories.

Pamela: That is so but I heard most of my stories from my mother. She was very good at telling stories.

Adeola: Do you keep an eye on the message of the stories?

Pamela: Yes, I do. All my stories are moral narratives.

Adeola: I gather you have written children's stories. Are they different from those ones?

Pamela: No, those are the same ones. But, as I said, adults enjoy them too.

Adeola: When you write are you particularly conscious of preserving certain kinds of images of black people?

Pamela: Yes, I am. The stories portray that consciousness. For example in my story about Rosa I choose a theme that will portray an African image. Rosa's present is a tree rather than a doll or sweets that children are normally given. I choose a fruit tree that will later bear fruits. Unfortunately, that book is not yet published. I wrote it at a time when we were talking all over the country about conservation and self-reliance. So I tried to put these ideas in a way that young people would understand. The book should have come out 2 years ago but it is still lying on somebody's desk. One worries about the relevance of the theme by the time the book is published, when it takes so long to bring it out.

Adeola: These are problems that can be tackled when we have viable publishing houses. Meanwhile, as a writer what do you consider to be your responsibility?

Pamela: Having taught before in a secondary school, and now working in a pre-school, I am familiar with people complaining that most of our reading books are written by people who do not know about us. When I write I am aware of these problems and I try not to repeat some of the mistakes.

Adeola: Can you be more specific? Are you talking about Africans who write like Europeans or those who are alienated from the grass-roots?

Pamela: I suppose you can describe it as alienation. So as to avoid irrelevance and alienation I often test my stories on my children. When I wrote *Rosa*, I read every section of it to my children, adjusting it according to their interest. The same is true of my other books.

Adeola: Can you tell me how you became interested in writing?

Pamela: When I was in high school, English was my best subject so I used to write during my free time. I wrote down the stories that I had heard. Then later, when I went to the University of Leicester in England, I wrote my thesis on African folktales, and that afforded me an opportunity to develop the interest I had before.

Adeola: Would you be interested in writing full time?

Pamela: I certainly wouldn't mind if I were sure that my books would be published. I've got a lot of materials right now but I don't feel the urge to write because the publishing is so slow.

Adeola: How can we deal with this problem of publishing?

Pamela: The only way is to have our own publishing houses.

Adeola: There are some publishing houses in England and America which publish only women writers. Is this the sort of development you are thinking about?

Pamela: That is the only way to solve our problem, if other people think as I do. We need African writers to read in the schools. All my shelves are still full of English writers. How can we get books if we don't get them published?

Adeola: Female writers are in the minority in Africa. Do you consider them to be a significant force in literature?

Pamela: If they do come out in their full force, they will be. As in every other field it is men who dominate, but women are coming out now. Education was given to men first. If you don't have the basic education, you are not exposed to other people in different spheres of life, how can you write? In addition, you need encouragement, which we women have not had. Most of the writers and critics are men and they don't pay much attention to what women write.

Adeola: The disadvantage that women suffer in education is being remedied.

Pamela: Yes, I agree with you that things have improved a great deal. In the first eight years of schooling here in Kenya, girls outnumber boys. The number of girls in the education system begins to dwindle as they move to the university level, because of the choice of subjects. It also depends on the country. If education is free, parents are compelled to send their children to school at least up to primary level. Parents still prefer sending boys to secondary school because they think the sons will help them, which is not always the case. If women are encouraged, particularly in literature, it will yield results. For it is the girls who are with their mothers collecting fire wood, cooking, etc. We do very well in writing because we have got the stuff. Boys don't tell stories when they are fighting!

Adeola: In your comments, so far, you have indicated some of the constraints that women experience as writers. Do you feel any of these constraints?

Pamela: No, in that respect I have been very lucky. It all comes very naturally to me, having chosen teaching as a career. And as far as marriage is concerned, so far so good, because I have married someone who understands. That goes a long way.

Adeola: In terms of understanding, what is your children's reaction to your being a writer?

Pamela: The whole family has been very supportive. As I mentioned earlier, when I was writing *Rosa* I used to read it to my children and my husband. They often suggested ideas here and there.

Adeola: Is there no serious constraint that you have experienced as a writer?

Pamela: No, if my books can be published, I'll spend all the time writing. If I say to my husband, 'I cannot come and help you today, I have something to write', he won't mind.

Adeola: How do the children react to your books?

Pamela: They are very proud of them. They are often anxious to see the books out, especially the ones they have participated in.

Adeola: Is any of your children interested in writing?

Pamela: I can't see that yet. My oldest is fifteen years old, seems to lean towards science. She wants to follow her father. My son is interested in craft, anything to do with his hands. Sewing has now been introduced in schools, and his work is very good, according to the teacher. He is not bothered by the fact that sewing is for girls. Even cookery he likes. He just enjoys these various things.

Adeola: Would you describe your creative process. How do you translate the stories you heard as a child into a book?

Pamela: To begin with, I didn't make the mistake of writing them in English. I wrote them first in my mother tongue, Dho-Luo, the language in which they were told to me. Then I selected ten of them and translated them into English. In the process of doing that I was able to see what fitted where, and consider how the children would react to them. That is where creativity comes in.

But in translation a lot of the meat is lost. It is the same in telling a story. When several people are telling a story the tenth person will not tell it as it is told to the first. I think it is worse in translation.

Adeola: Do you feel the need to write materials focused on the needs of girls and women?

Pamela: I won't say it is very necessary, but it can be done. It is true that there are few models in books for girls because heroes have always been men. This discrimination has always been there and it is for us to change it. That is why we need more women writers.

Adeola: Somebody says that women are not good scientists because it is just men that are portrayed in these fields. Children are psychologically affected by what they see.

Pamela: I agree with that reasoning, although I must say I wasn't aware of this bias when I was at school. Now that people are open about it we realise this is how it has always been. As convenor for Education and Curriculum Development, I spotted the tendency to present the image of women as servants or second to men in most writings. Conscious effort to change this situation is being recommended.

Adeola: Are you a nursery school teacher because you love storytelling?

Pamela: I started being interested in storytelling when I was very young. I grew with it. I used to gather children together and tell them stories. Being a Sunday school teacher I enjoyed telling bible stories, so you could say I grew with it before I could think of becoming a nursery school teacher.

Adeola: In this nursery school, is story-telling a significant part of instruction?

Pamela: Yes, every day we have a story-telling session at the latter part of the day, like at home when stories are told as you have your last *Uji* (porridge). Sometimes I alternate. I tell the children some stories first thing in the morning and see how they react. I have encouraged mothers to come so that we don't listen to the same person all the time. Mothers who go to the *shambas* (farms) could be brought in and given some shillings to tell the children some stories. We seem to tell only Cinderella stories, we need to tell our own. In my school days, two or three children would be asked to tell stories every day. It was part of the school curriculum.

Adeola: Is there any women writers' organisation that you know of?

Pamela: No. We had a Kenya Writers Association which died a few years ago. Someone is reviving it but it is not exclusively for women. A Kenya Oral Literature Association was born three years ago out of the Unesco conference on 'Young Writers'. It did not focus on oral literature alone, but we just saw the need for more research and dissemination of ideas.

Adeola: Were there many young women at that conference?

Pamela: Not really.

Adeola: My primary objective is to find out how we can get more women writing. There are many men writers, but do they represent our interests?

Pamela: No, they do not. But then how do you encourage women to write more. It has to come from deep down in the self. The schools can help by teaching creative writing, encouraging the inclusion of good books by women as compulsory reading. An association of women writers would be useful.

Adeola: What would be your advice to young women who are interested in writing?

Pamela: I would tell them to write and not stop. We must ensure that things written that are of publishable quality will be published. There will be frustrations, such as my experience with *Rosa*, which I wrote on an issue that was contemporary then. The publishing house has frustrated all my efforts by their delay in publishing it. However, the main thing is to keep writing. Hopefully, with all the new attention on women, we will have a greater means of recording our voices through more publications.

Ellen Kuzwayo

Ellen Kuzwayo was born in South Africa and received her education in that country, where she attended the University of the Witwatersrand for a degree in Social Work. She has been a school teacher and social worker. She came into writing in her sixties with the publication of *Call Me Woman* (1985), her autobiography. The book also pays tribute to many unacknowledged heroic women. She is active in the community life of Soweto and has won several honours among her people. Apart from her writing, she has helped to make two films: *Awake from Mourning* and *Tsiamelo*, ('A Place of Goodness').

5

Ellen Kuzwayo

This interview was conducted at the Conference on the Black Woman Writer and the Diaspora, East Lansing, Michigan, 27–30 October 1985.

Adeola: Your autobiography *Call Me Woman* is really about the history and sufferings of your people in South Africa. This seems to contradict the statement that writing is a lonely act. What would you say to this?

Ellen: I would really differ. Maybe in certain settings writing may be an isolated act. But in my setting, in South Africa, I did not find it lonely. In fact, I was challenged by the lives of so many, many women, who have made such tremendous contribution to the development and growth of our country, in particular, to the development of the black woman. As a result I find myself inspired all the time. In fact, when the publishing process of the book was coming to an end, I noticed that the publishers had edited so many women out. I had to tell them to push me out of my book and put the women in because those were the people who inspired me to write the book. Those were the women who gave me support right through the writing. Their lives became so powerful for me. Some of them have long been dead, but their lives are still very much felt in the community because of the impact and contribution they made.

Adeola: Do you regard your book as a kind of celebration of the heroic struggle of women in South Africa?

Ellen: Yes, indeed I regard my book as a celebration of the women, whose achievement is exposed at the international level for people to know about. I always felt there was this great heroic contribution and achievement by women, but nobody knows about it outside the country, and maybe even within the country. Because of the structure of society, with women right at the bottom, they did not come out to be seen as the real motivating element in the lives of the people, of the country as a whole.

Adeola: You are suggesting that women are the real motivating element in the struggle for liberation?

Ellen: Yes, they are the real motivating element in the struggle.

Adeola: Now, what about the next generation? It would really be begging the question to ask if you are concerned about the fate of the future generation as a writer. I know you are concerned, but how would you explain your concern?

Ellen: At the close of my book, I end up lamenting the heritage that the world is leaving, that my country is leaving for the youth of that country. When I think of my grandchildren and the children of their age group, I would weep if I knew that after all the struggles, they are still going to live the kind of life that I have lived in my country. And I feel that today, every country, and every sane, thinking, mature adult, should begin to put the record straight for the future life of the younger generation. I say it in South Africa, I will say it in Africa and I will go out and say it on the international scene: we owe it to the younger generation.

Adeola: How do we put the record straight?

Ellen: I think there has been far too much undermining of the feelings, the opinions, the thinking of the young people. We have always believed that we have the answer to all the problems in the world. But, do we?. Do we? Maybe we need to stop for a while and assess the contribution we have made in the past. Further, in a very objective way we need to assess the contribution made by the younger generation in the 1960's, 1970's and 1980's, and without prejudice come up with our discoveries and findings.

Adeola: Are there young people writing in South Africa?

Ellen: The young people in South Africa, most of them are not writing books. They are much more in drama, their feelings come out much more on the stage. I think they feel the tension so much that they cannot discipline themselves to sit down and write. So they come in a group and what they express they express because they are full of tension and they want to say it *now*. A book takes too long. And they want to sing it, they want to dramatize it and they want to be very angry on the stage. This is what I see today happening in South Africa, as with Poppy Nongena, the play of a woman who portrays the life of the black family in South Africa. It is a very interesting play. She lives in it. I think this is what the young generation is concerned about. They can't discipline themselves to write a book which takes them years of research and of putting down on paper. The anger is in them, it must come out *now*. They must express it. They must tell the world about it. But the play is not allowed to be performed in our country. The government is arresting them and putting them in jail. They don't appreciate this great play.

Adeola: Of course not. How can they appreciate it when it portrays their evil deeds?

Ellen: Indeed, it portrays their doings so powerfully.

Adeola: To be black and to be a woman is a double ill fate. What is your response to this?

Ellen: I don't know why you want me to answer this because I have every reason to believe that every woman, every black woman, particularly in Africa, is fully aware of this. In the process of growing up we encounter it. In school we were told that we couldn't do certain subjects, that certain subjects were good for certain people. I think this has given women a double exclusion from all sorts of sources. We've always been stereotyped and I think it is this stereotyping that has given the black woman an extra burden, as a black and as a woman.

Adeola: You have not had any difficulty with publishing your book, have you?

Ellen: This is what has come as a great surprise to me. When I hear of the struggles of other writers being rejected by publishers, I am amazed at my comparatively happy experience. One publisher accepted my manuscript. Then the first publisher who had rejected me, wanted me back.

Adeola: Have you found fulfilment in writing?

Ellen: I want to tell you that previously I lived with my emotional pain: the tensions of my first marriage that broke up, the tensions of the son that was taken away from me, the tensions when my aunt sent me away from home, all these I lived with and sometimes I didn't want to talk about them. I was shutting them up inside me because I felt people might laugh at me. Then suddenly I wrote, and when I was writing the tension floated onto the pen and it has released me. Today I can discuss every aspect of my life with no question and no shame.

Adeola: And many people are learning great lessons from your experiences.

Ellen: Yes, because now I can share with young people. I can say to them, 'Do not worry about things. I don't have to worry about that. There are greater things in life'. The achievement of writing has given me another level of fulfilment and another level of liberation.

Adeola: It is a great encouragement for others, women especially. Of course, you plan to continue writing?

Ellen: Yes, of course, I plan to.

Adeola: How long did it take you to write *Call Me Woman*?

Ellen: It took me three and a half years.

Adeola: How did you combine writing with your taxing duties as a social worker?

Ellen: Oh! I had to get away from regular employment and work with women on a voluntary basis so that they could respect my time; also to make sure that I was not stealing the time of my employer. Then I looked for sponsorship to pay my typists and to give myself a little bit of bread. This enabled me to write as an independent person, not as an employed person.

Adeola: For how many hours a day did you work on your book?

Ellen: I went to work at half past eight in the morning like everybody else and clocked out at half past four in the afternoon like everybody else. I was writing all day, and sometimes I was out on field work for my research to make sure that all the texts in the book were authentic.

Adeola: What barriers, both inward and outward, did you face in attempting to write?

Ellen: Maybe the very first barrier I experienced is the one I talked about yesterday. It took me long to have confidence to write. I didn't believe I could do it. Of course, one other thing was the fact that I needed money. I considered, 'If I leave my job how am I going to live?' Those were the two major problems that I faced, obstacles that were in me, that kept on saying, 'Ellen you can't do it'. Then when I finished my dissertation at the university I said, 'Lord, if I can do this I think I can write a book'. There were barriers outside as well, such as writing to institutions for information and data I needed to check against before writing. Some of the universities, I must say, 70–80 per cent of the universities that I approached, both the ethnic ones as well as the 'open' universities which had a few white students, were very co-operative. I came across only one or two which withheld information and refused to respond to what I wanted. That satisfied me a great deal. Maybe one other thing was the question of travelling long distances to get the information that I wanted. I think the thing that helped also was that, at that time, they were producing the film *Tsiamelo* ('Place of Goodness'), which was related to my book. So I benefitted a great deal from the research that was done for the film. It fulfilled a great need in the research area.

Adeola: Virginia Woolf said, 'I do my best work and feel most braced with my back to the wall. It's an odd feeling though, writing against the current: difficult entirely to disregard the current.'[1] How do you relate to this statement? Is it also true of your own creative experience?

Ellen: I think this can be interpreted in terms of time. When you are sponsored, you know that your sponsorship will come to an end and you have to work with speed to achieve what you are doing. You also have to realise that, in South Africa, in particular, if a black person fails, it is used as a generalization that we are all failures. If you succeed, then they say, 'She is wonderful'. So I wanted to debunk that myth that black people never do anything to its completion. But I had to produce the very best, to prove that what they are saying is a question of not giving people opportunity; rather than the stereotype, that the fault lies with the people.

Adeola: Do you agree that the writer is the product of her historical circumstances and that material conditions are of crucial importance?

Ellen: Yes, I would say that is very true. I think that in the context, one could say that all black people are where they are, whether they have failed to reach maximum achievement or whether they have remained stagnant and never made any effort, because of the history of their countries. We have never had support to achieve and succeed, and we have also been denied certain material things that could facilitate us as individuals. In some cases those in power have taken it even from your family which could have helped you. They always make you feel like you are going to get it tomorrow. They want you to accept it as pie in the sky, after death you will get it. They don't realise that you are as human as they are and you want to get it now, you need it now. They have it, why can't you have it?

Note

1. Virginia Woolf: Introduction to *Women and Writing* (UK: The Woman's Press, 1979), p. 4.

Muthoni Likimani

Muthoni Likimani was born and educated to secondary level in Kenya. She was formerly a popular broadcaster and producer until she got involved in writing. Writing full time, however, does not fulfil her, so she has an advertising and promotion business in Nairobi. Her publications include *Women in Kenya, They Shall be Chastized, What Does a Man Want, Shangazi na Watoto* and *Passbook Number F47927: Women and Mau Mau in Kenya*. They are all works of fiction. In the last, and most ambitious, she examines the most difficult period in Kenya's history, the Mau Mau revolutionary war, from the point of view of the women's contribution. This book forms a useful link with Micere Githae Mugo's play (co-authored with Ngugi wa Thiong'o) on the same subject, *The Trial of Dedan Kimathi*.

6
Muthoni Likimani

This interview was conducted in Nairobi on 25 June 1986.

Adeola: Can you tell me how you became a writer?

Muthoni: Encouragement is necessary for many people. I knew when I was at school that I was a storyteller and an observer. I used to write even then, whenever I observed an issue.

However, it was a West Indian who encouraged me to write. I think he was a Trinidadian. I was a broadcaster, and this man started talking to me about writing. He insisted that he must see what I wrote. I think he was a doctor of medicine. I felt what I was writing was rubbish but he insisted. He said to me, 'Muthoni, you must write. Type what you write as it is – don't change it'. That was how I became bold and have continued writing till now.

Adeola: How long have you been writing?

Muthoni: Quite a number of years. Right now I have five books published. One needs time and good surroundings, and with some encouragement one develops confidence. I feel there is not enough information about the business of writing. Some people even think you need money to write, they don't know you are paid.

Adeola: Is anything being done to reach out to young writers?

Muthoni: I don't think so. We have to use whatever approach we can to encourage young women to write.

Adeola: What subjects do you write about?

Muthoni: I write about society. I suppose I write as a woman. For example, one of my books is entitled *What Does a Man Want*? It is a frivolous book. In it I portray some contradictions – if you are old the men want young girls, if you are young they think you don't have much sense. If you love them too much they think you are possessive, they get fed up. These are the problems of married life that I am trying to project. That book has turned out to be very successful. It is very popular and it has been translated into German. I have another book entitled *They Shall Be Chastised*. I grew up in a church environment; my father was a canon. I had wished to title the book *Confusion*, but my publisher objected. From that title you can guess what the book is about.

My third and most important book is *Passbook Number F 47927*. That was my identity number during the Mau Mau struggle. I could be considered a freedom fighter. The book is about the contribution women made through very severe sufferings. Their sufferings can be compared with what Mandela is going through today.

Adeola: Could you tell me people's reaction to it?

Muthoni: It has been very well received. Previously the younger generation felt they didn't know what was happening. But now they think they are being informed. It is the first book by someone who was not in the forest, but contributed in a different way.

Adeola: Do you think that a book like that encourages people to respect women?

Muthoni: Yes, of course. That is what was intended. You see, the younger generation respect their fathers for what they contributed to what they have today. Generally, they knew nothing about the role their mothers played in the liberation struggle. For my part, I did not contribute directly because I was in a mission and Mau Mau was not in my area. I married young and had babies so I didn't go fighting. But there were many women who got involved and one cannot ignore their contribution.

Adeola: When you write, are you conscious of preserving certain images of the African?

Muthoni: I am a very frank person, when I write I let myself go. I write to unearth an issue. Once I write it out I am satisfied. I don't try to answer any question directly. For example, it can be said that *Passbook Number F 47927* indirectly answers the question: Did women contribute to the Mau Mau struggle? In all the previous literature on the subject nobody ever focused on the contribution of women. We read about men in detention, but nobody said there was also a gang of women guerillas fighting, carrying guns, hiding and feeding the Mau Mau. Even the prostitutes incited the white soldiers and got their guns after getting their men to beat them. These women made their own contribution, and they were reliable spies. Yet nobody talks about them.

Adeola: As a mother, grandmother, someone involved in the political life of Kenya and also a writer, how do you integrate these various aspects of your life?

Muthoni: My children are now grown up. My baby is 24 years of age, so I am free. I like writing very early in the morning, between 4 and 10 a.m. Then I go to my office. On Saturdays I attend to my personal affairs – washing, cooking, resting and seeing friends.

People often complain about time, but time is no excuse for not writing, it is only a question of organisation. You must be disciplined to the point of being a nuisance – unhook your telephone. Sometimes very early in the morning I disconnect my telephone because it is quiet and I want to write. Personal talk is for after 4 p.m. African women are tough people. They work and collect degrees, sometimes when they are big and pregnant. We are very tough people, aren't we?

Adeola: We are amazing people, really. In spite of all the odds against us, we still manage to do a lot, and our writers should celebrate these achievements. Can you say something about your creative process. How do you create a book?

Muthoni: That depends upon the individual, the way your mind works. I don't think you can be trained. Some people say to me, 'Write me something about this' (lifting an ash tray). Some people in response might write ten sentences, others a whole book. Your own creative process is the way your mind works.

Adeola: Do you think the women's movement has had an impact on African women writers?

Muthoni: No, I don't think so. The women's movement in Kenya concentrates more on the uneducated than on the educated ones. They try to educate women on hygiene, income generation and other developmental projects.

Adeola: Would you wish to devote your time entirely to writing?

Muthoni: Maybe later. Right now, I am trying to train others to do my work in this office. With creative writing, sometimes you don't have the head for writing. That is why I don't do that alone, so that, when I don't feel like writing, I can do something else.

Adeola: What work do you do apart from writing?

Muthoni: I have done several things in my time. First of all, I was a teacher. Then through teaching I started broadcasting. When I was an education student in England, I was involved in educational broadcasting, including advertizing. I now do market promotion and publication of periodicals. I have a company which publishes the *Kenya Food Directory, Fashion and Beauty*. I promote other companies. I rarely publish novels, they are difficult to sell. Since the Women's Decade celebration, I have been doing Women Programme Network on the radio. These are a few of the things that I am involved in.

Adeola: Do these various activities feed your creative impulse?

Muthoni: Not really. They are just business, income generating activities, if you like.

Adeola: The fact that you have to do so many other things besides writing implies that a woman cannot be independent as a writer.

Muthoni: Writing doesn't pay easily. If you need money you have to do other things. The last book is doing very well so I am encouraged to write more. In fact I have started on something else.

Adeola: What is the response of your family and friends to your being a writer?

Muthoni: They like it. My children are very proud.

Adeola: You mentioned that you have more time to write now. How did you manage in the earlier years when your children were young?

Muthoni: I did not write then. I concentrated on the home. Besides, it was not convenient to write. My husband was a doctor and we moved around a lot. I tried to write but it was very difficult.

Adeola: What is your advice to women who wish to write?

Muthoni: If they have any material, if they feel they have a message, they must just put it down as I used to do. They must seek advice, show what they write to publishers. They might be discouraged at first but they must keep trying and they must not give up. They must also read widely because you cannot be a good writer without reading. In Africa, we need children's books. As it is, we are still using a lot of western books that are sometimes not quite relevant to our situation, to say the least.

Adeola: Have you experienced any difficulty in publishing your works?

Muthoni: Not really. It is difficult to start, but when they know you it is not so bad. Understandably, they take you with caution the first time. Now, publishers ring me up and ask for manuscripts. However, to make the breakthrough is not very easy. You know, it is a business, the publishers do not want to tie down their money, they want to sell. So you have to persevere if they reject your work, and keep trying.

Adeola: Do you see any differences in the ways African male and female writers handle theme?

Muthoni: It must be different. Men by nature are hard. Women are thinkers, they are feminine, they are ladies, they are soft. They approach things in a soft way. Men will talk about war, politics; women will write about the family. I have not read enough women writers in order to be able to make more valid comparisons.

Adeola: What writers have interested you?

Muthoni: I like quite a few. I have read a lot of West African writers; Achebe and others. I like African writers more than any others, but occasionally I read other writers. I like books that deal with issues.

Adeola: Does the consideration that publishers want books that sell determine your themes?

Muthoni: A writer writes what touches her mind. Established writers know what sells. That consideration doesn't determine, for the writer, what to write, but it does for the publisher. It is nice if you can combine both – that is, write something which you can sell and through which you can also pass on a message.

Molara Ogundipe-Leslie

Molara Ogundipe-Leslie is from western Nigeria. She was educated at Queen's School, Ede and the University of Ibadan (then
University College), where she graduated with first class honours
in English. She has taught English and African literature in
universities in Nigeria and the USA. A contemporary of most of
our leading male writers, like Wole Soyinka and J.P. Clark, and
critics, like Abiola Irele, she has been part of the movement to
develop a criticism that will match the stature of the creative
literature of Africa. Her insightful assessment of Amos Tutuola's
writing was one of the earliest to restore Tutuola to his proper
place in African literature, as a founding father and a visionary.
Her critical articles have been published in various journals,
on subjects like African aesthetics, and appraisals of the work
of various writers, like Chinua Achebe, Wole Soyinka and
Christopher Okigbo. Recently, she has been occupied with giving
a Marxist reading to African literature. She is concerned about
women's issues and at present is with the Directorate for Social
Mobilization as an adviser to the Nigerian Government on the
mobilization of women. *Sew the Old Days* (1985) is her only
published collection of poetry.

7

Molara Ogundipe-Leslie

Adeola: As one of the most serious African female critics, what have been your preoccupations?

Molara: The development of Africa, not in the sense of western imperialist development theory, but in terms of what will make the continent richer, healthier, safer and more dignified for all her peoples, not only people of a particular class. This means I have been concerned with our pre–colonial past and what made it possible for us to be colonized; our colonial experience and its ravages on our lands and our psyche. It means I have been concerned with the quality of life of our people as individuals, and the condition of the woman in Africa. I have also been very interested in alternative modes of modernizing and enriching Africa other than being in a dependent economy, hence my explorations of other ideologies and social formations than capitalist liberalism. I have also worked with peace movements in the conviction that we need the world to survive before we can realize any dreams. European feminists in the peace movement also have a great deal of political and technological information which is useful to us as African women without libraries or archives.

Adeola: Most people have complained that cricitism has not matched creative output in African literature. What do you consider to be responsible for this?

Molara: Perhaps because the criticism of African literature was done by enthusiasts in the early days and perhaps because African literature in the metropolitan languages was itself the child of a small class of people, themselves marginalized in the culture and sometimes foreign to Africa. It took a while for African literature to become 'respectable' and legitimized in African university circles. But since the 1970's, it can be said that quite a deal of fine criticism in English has been done, in particular by critics from Ghana, Nigeria, Kenya, Uganda and Sierra Leone. Francophone African criticism also has its big names.

Adeola: In the 1970's, you published an article on African aesthetics. Could you tell us what are your current views on this subject?

Molara: I have not been able to pursue the guidelines on African aesthetics because I came home to Nigeria and became swamped by teaching, consciousness–raising and feminist research and activitism. It is a work, however, which I hope to come back to sometime soon with the maturity and information one has been able to gain over the years. Certain issues are clear, such as that there is no one 'African' aesthetic; that to study indigenous aesthetics we must look at discrete communities and cultures each of which has its own aesthetic universe: the Yoruba as opposed to the Tiv or the Gikuyu or the Tutsis. Then we must attempt to elicit the aesthetic criteria of the people themselves and not impose European ideas, as was done to African sculpture. We must also bear in mind that the traditional universe itself is not static.

Adeola: You are trying to develop a Marxist critical approach to African literature. Has this effort been stimulated by your view of the function of art in African society?

Molara: Yes, indeed. My view has been stimulated by the Marxist view that art has a cognitive role, that the Sidneyean 'teaching and pleasing' implies values and ideas inherent in the work. And since one also sees art as a midwife to history, as it were, it is very important what art says and how it helps to move people towards the ideal of a just and scientifically advanced society.

Adeola: I have known you for over two decades, during which we have watched the rise and fall of the Nigerian society, through the turbulence of a civil war and a series of coup d'etats. How have these experiences affected you as a female literary critic?

Molara: The experiences of the past two decades cannot but affect one. We in Nigeria in 1987 are still having to confront the consequences of the fratricidal civil war. We are confronting economically the aftermath of the oil boom – the mad waste of our petroleum resources in the 1970's. Now we face the Structural Adjustment Programme after having rejected the IMF loan. And the people seem to be stewing in a hotter juice. My sojourn in Lagos as a member of the editorial board of *The Guardian* newspaper afforded me a chance to see the acute impact of our political and economic realities on the urban people. It is almost a hermetic situation for the poor, maddening at times.

Adeola: What have been the most crucial periods of your life as a writer and critic?

Molara: Crucial periods? Perhaps leaving university and having to make decisions for myself for the first time after having lived a very sheltered life. Falling in love, being married, childbirth and child-care, living and teaching in the U.S. during the late 1960's and early 1970's, in the hey day of the youth, black and feminist movements; returning to a changed Nigeria which was now more callous and materialistic than we dreamed in our idealistic lectures in the US. You see, the personal is indivisible from the creative.

Adeola: What has being a woman and a writer meant to you – joy, heartaches or increased strength to struggle on?

Molara: Being a writer is cathartic. It relieves you of some of the anguish of living and the tension of what I describe in one of my poems as, 'living and finely living. Living on the fine nerves of our knowing'. It makes you feel your life is somehow worthwhile. In a strange way, too, you feel less alone. Not loneliness but aloneness. Loneliness is different from aloneness. I never feel lonely because my world is studded with people I love, my books, my music, my concerns, my aspirations, my various projects, my dreams.

Adeola: Is the African woman writer, in your opinion, different from her counterparts elsewhere?

Molara: I don't know if the African woman writer is different from women writers in other parts of the world. I can only hazard some guesses based on what I know to be some of the facts of the existence of the African woman writer. Because of the definitely patriarchal arrangements of the society, publicly and privately, most women bear a double workload, if not a triple one. Hence they have even less time and leisure than their western counterparts to think or write. African society may welcome women writers, but it would certainly be shocked if they handled certain subjects on which western writers have now gained the freedom to be vocal. A woman will probably be expected to write mainly for children or to be edifying in general, since the malefolk seem to feel the responsibility for the nation's morals rests solely on her shoulders. She is falsely grandified with this task while all around she is discriminated against, excluded from real power, exploited at all levels and derided most of the time in the society. She is also usually seen as the cause of whatever happens negatively in the country. The national scapegoat. The cause of the nation's decline.

Adeola: By your article, 'The Female Writer and her Commitment', you have added your voice to the feminist debate. What impact has this worldwide concern about women's position as an oppressed person had on our very male–oriented society?

Molara: The effect of the worldwide concern about the woman's position in Nigeria has been varied. I intend to write about it more fully in another place. It is as to be expected multi-faceted and contradictory when it is not totally false and misleading. The male-dominated society reacts in the usual sexist fashion by denying that there is any oppression of women in Africa; glorifying an unknown precolonial past where our African mothers were totally happy; accusing conscious women activists of being victims of western ideas and copycats of white women; claiming that 'the family' is more important than the fate of the individual woman; brushing aside women's concerns with the hyprocrisy that 'national development' is a greater priority now than women's liberation; asserting that women anyhow do not need to be liberated because they have never been in bondage. So you have a compounding of historical and sociological falsification, all to the end of frightening women into quietude. The most vocal and courageous who continue to talk and act socially and politically are stigmatised.

Adeola: What are your views on scholarship and underdevelopment, particularly in relation to women who try to be scholars, writers, academics and mothers at the same time?

Molara: Scholarship is extremely crucial in an underdeveloped society, because we need information about yesterday and today in order to build the future. We have a continent full of illiterate and uninformed people to bring into the modern world. A woman who is serious and is involved must be a 'scholar' in its pristine sense of 'one who studies' not in the sense of degree holder. It is, as you know, triply hard for the woman who wants to be a scholar, a writer, academic and mother. I should really say quadruply hard. Perhaps this is why African women writers are less productive and those who are, live in special family arrangements. Flora Nwapa told me that Buchi Emecheta said she stopped having children when she stopped having babies!

Adeola: Am I correct in saying that African women scholars and professionals, as a group, are not taken seriously? Is the view still current that women belong in the kitchen and those, who do not see washing nappies and cooking as the essential business of their lives, are eccentrics? In your own experience have you encountered such backward attitudes?

Molara: Yes, unfortunately, African women scholars and professionals are not taken seriously. Most men still take women's jobs as hobbies for them; nothing serious or self-defining, just something to do outside the home to help the family income. And if you are a married professional, it is felt you do not need promotion or salary increases because you have a husband who caters for you anyway. And your male colleagues may be envious of your husband who has two heavy pay–packets to use – yours and his – so they take their anger or envy out on you.

Adeola: As a literary scholar you inspired the re–evaluation of Amos Tutuola's contribution to African literature, changing the view that saw him as a noble savage, a 'primitive' artist, to that of the pioneer of a rich literary tradition. What would you consider to be your other major contributions?

Molara: My contribution has been mainly through public lectures on African aesthetics; my insistence in my teaching at the University of Ibadan on an African perspective on issues; my production for over a decade of students with an Africa–centred vision; my involvement in feminist debates and the search for African feminist literary theories; my research on the condition of African women and the study of realism in Amos Tutuola. (A surprising idea, since Tutuola seems to be the very antithesis of realism. But I shall find it interesting to prove my point.)

Adeola: What is your opinion on the contribution of women to African literature and literary scholarship?

Molara: African women have contributed quite substantially to African theatre and fiction. I wonder why those two genres, and not so much to poetry? In criticism, new voices are rising and you will find they are more of the under–50 generation. This has to do with when women began to receive university education or engage in scholarship. Every evaluation of women's contribution we make must be done in terms of the proportionate number given the opportunity to contribute; when, historically, women had the chance to function in such circles.

Adeola: In your article that I cited earlier, you refer with approval to Simone de Beauvoir's statement:

> Man reserves for himself the terrors and triumphs of transcendence; he offers woman safety, the temptations of passivity and acceptance; he tells her that passivity and acceptance are her nature. Simone de Beauvoir tells her that is a lie, that her nature is complicated and various, that she must escape, liberate herself, shape her own future, deny the myths that confine her.

In your own personal life how have you managed to liberate yourself from the myths that confine you as an African woman? How do you see us in comparison with our mothers' generation?

Molara: In comparison with our mothers' generation, we are less fatalistic about women's condition. I feel, however, that the average middle class woman still values marrige and children over and above everything. Hence she is willing to accept any humiliation from a difficult husband. In that, she is not different from our mothers, and don't forget that women like you and I are not the norm. We are not in the majority. I make the class distinction though because so-called illiterate women have less of a mystique about marriage, the institution and the husband. They will divorce in a flash over practical things like money for food, clothes, sex etc. which they feel are their dues from their husbands. There is a higher divorce rate at the rural and low income levels, and more changing of partners, because for them, marriage is a pragmatic arrangement, and I think their attitude is much healthier.

Now, my own personal life. Liberating myself from the myths that confine us is an on-going process. One is often surprised at certain reactions in oneself which emerge or lurk in the crevices of one's psyche. I have always reacted to discrimination against women since I observed it in primary school and all around. I always wanted the best and saw that only in competing with men (and beating them too) can you get exposure to the best. I have benefitted from my upbringing, my conscious mother, reading progressive and left literature, feminist writings and historical documentation of women's lives. Mainly, it has been a lived experience, of trial and error. A trial through torture, because life itself forces you to decisions. You encounter a situation and your very being reacts against it. You resent the indignity to the very soul of your being and you know you are willing to die for your refusal. That is how I liberated myself. Also to know that work liberates, that as the Yorubas say, 'The palms of your hands never betray you' for much of the acceptance of indignity by women is the fear of not being supported, of losing food and shelter and later their children. Children are used to blackmail women unconsciously.

Adeola: You could be accused of idealising African womanhood in your description of the wife in *The Palm-wine Drinkard* (UK: Faber, 1952) as:

> One of the best and most correct images of the Yoruba woman of all classes: a courageous, resourceful woman who dares situations with her husband, who works at anything and willingly changes roles with him, where the need arises.[2]

Do you find such qualities among educated African women? Is that your ideal of African womanhood?

Molara: That is my ideal of the married African woman. There are other kinds of African women. Yes, I find such qualities among educated African women. They do a great deal for their husbands and children; sacrifice what they have in cash and kind, only for them to be cast aside later or forced into polygamy with younger women as new wives.

Adeola: I would like to engage you in answering those profound questions you pose at the end of your article, 'The Female Writer and her Commitment'. You ask, 'Is there anything that recommends the female writer more particularly to this socially educative role? Does the African female writer have any moral prerogative to point the way to others and educate the spirit? And why? As mothers, more experienced sufferers or more sentient and ethical beings?'

Molara: I would say that certain things need to be said. That the critic is also a teacher, in Achebe's sense – someone who points out things which may have been missed or could be missed. We are closer to human need and suffering through the experiences of motherhood and womanhood. We gain more compassionate hearts thereby and history has shown that women demonstrate more probity and commitment in situations of responsibility.

Adeola: I note you have published some poems. When did you start writing poetry?

Molara: I wrote some poetry as a student at the University of Ibadan in the late 1950's and 1960's. I have always scribbled. Since I was thirteen or fourteen I have written short stories, novels and comic books. A group of us in secondary school once started a comic book which the headmistress, who was English, approved. Boarding school was so strict in those days. Things had to be judged worthy. I forget how the whole effort got diffused. I now have a book of poems published under the title: *Sew the Old Days and Other Poems* by Evans Publishers in 1985. The manuscript went out in 1980.

Adeola: Would you like to describe your writing process? Is writing poetry the same as writing criticism?

Molara: My writing process. Hm! There are several, depending on the subject, the situation and my state of mind. Sometimes I take notes, write down snatches of phrases, things, issues and objects which strike me. I may sit down to write a poem later. Sometimes I write the poem all at once as the thoughts come and then tinker later. I have also woken up one morning to find the poem completely written in my head. I woke up with the refrain on my lips, 'And there are here the errors of the rendering'. I sat down and simply put down the poem. Always, a lot of tinkering and re-arrangement and rewriting of lines come later. I am rather fastidious about rhythm. I think rhythm is the key to the poetic nature of a poem. As important as thought.

For prose or academic writing, I find I have to read a great deal. I read the text and other writing bearing on the text. Then I let some time pass, hours or a day. Sometimes, I sleep and when I wake up, things have fallen into place and I proceed to tackle the job. I find sleep a great mental restorative. I also find that with mental overload of reading a lot of things, ingesting a lot of information and encountering different and contrary views, sleeping over it all, helps rest my mind and settle everything in place. I wake up renewed and strong to impose my own pattern of perception on all the data.

Adeola: What lessons would you like to pass on to those who will come after us – particularly our daughters?

Molara: Waow, you are one for difficult and weighty questions. For our daughters, I would like to insist they appreciate the dignity of labour and see that no-one exploits their labour. They should know that in self-reliance, in that crude but first principle of being able to feed oneself, lies the kernel of self-determination and dignity. The

Yorubas say and my mother likes to say: 'Once your hand reaches your mouth, the rest is minor'. They must seek relationships that are not asymmetrical; never be at a disadvantage willingly in anything. Never be a masochist. Find husbands who are their friends first and then their life–long partners and playmates. Loving should be fun and self–improving not self–reducing and servile. They should interest themselves in things of the mind and the spirit. When everything else fails, a working mind and self-reliant hands will see them through. As mothers and patriots, they should be interested in the building up of their nations.

Adeola: As a critic, are you fully satisfied with the development of African literature and its response to the needs of our society?

Molara: Yes, a literature cannot be artificially developed. People all over the continent are responding to the realities of life in terms of their needs. There is a lot of writing going on in Nigeria today, poetry, fiction, drama, magazines, neswpapers, etc. Every day it seems a new magazine or newspaper comes out and they are in great demand.

Adeola: At the risk of sounding repetitive, but in the hope that one might come across an original and helpful answer – why is it that in the field of literature as in almost all other fields the African woman's voice is muted if not completely disregarded? Why is it that we have no women to compare with an Achebe, a Soyinka, an Ngugi and an Irele?

Molara: Perhaps I answered that earlier by saying that women have less time, less leisure and less preparation for writing. Women spend their time waiting on others and managing other people – their husband, their children and other older relatives and visitors – in addition to managing their own lives. Where a man can withdraw into his study to write, a woman usually cannot.

Adeola: Do you really feel that these men speak for us?

Molara: These men cannot speak for us. And they should not be expected to. Only rounded human beings who consciously seek wholeness in human society and life; who know that society can progress only with the full recognition of men and women both, and not women ministering to men and living through men; only such whole men can speak for women. And such men should not only theorize about woman's place and role, they should also live out their theories in their personal lives.

Adeola: What are your views on men as critics of women's writing?

Molara: Usually patronising and legislative. Many feel the concerns of women are not serious enough since they are about the area of emotions and the private life. I wonder how we got the idea in colonised societies that only political themes are respectable. A cultural lag from colonial times perhaps? Great literature has always been about human emotions and the actions which spring from them. *Anna Karenina* is first and foremost a love story; *Crime and Punishment* is about the psychology of a young man in a specific situation. But no; these are not respectable themes in Africa. Well, I am not knocking politics. I only feel the critical attitude amputates a very basic and central part of African life.

Notes

1. Molara Ogundipe-Leslie: article on African aesthetics in *Journal of the New African Literature and the Arts*, 1974.
2. Molara Ogundipe-Leslie, re *The Palm-wine Drinkard* in B. Lindfors (ed), *Critical Perspectives in Amos Tutuola* (London: HEB, 1980).

Penina Muhando

Penina Muhando was born in Tanzania in 1948. She received all her education from primary to tertiary level in Tanzania. She holds a B.A. in theatre arts, an M.A. in education and a Ph.D. in language and linguistics from the University of Dar-es-Salaam. The challenge posed by her desire to communicate first and foremost with her Tanzanian and East African audience has led to her choice of writing, so far, only in Kiswahili. She is aware of the restriction this imposes on the circulation of her works but is willing to pay the price. Meanwhile, her works continue to show maturity as her popularity grows among her home audience. She is committed to writing plays that are directly concerned with social and developmental problems as the title of the plays indicate: *Hatia* ('Guilt'); *Tambuene Haki Zetu* ('Recognize Our Rights'); *Heshima Yangu* ('My Respect'); *Pambo* ('Decoration'); *Talaka si mke wangu* ('Woman, I Divorce You'); *Nguzo-mama* ('Mother Pillar'); and *Harakati za Ukombozi* ('Liberation Struggles'), co-authored with Lihamba and Balisidya. She is presently professor and head of the Department of Theatre Arts at the University of Dar-es-Salaam.

8
Penina Muhando

This interview was conducted at the University of Dar-es-Salaam, on Monday 7 July 1986.

Adeola: I have known you since the late 1960's, when I lived in Dar-es-Salaam and you were a student. I was, therefore, very excited when, at a conference I attended last October in East Lansing, Michigan on Black Women Writers and the Diaspora, I learnt that you have published several plays. In fact, a paper was presented on your plays. That paper was just informative as none of the participants had read your plays which are all written in Kiswahili. You have obviously taken a deliberate decision to write in Kiswahili as all your nine plays are written in that language. How do you feel about excluding all your other African sisters who do not know Kiswahili?

Penina: I really wish I could write in a language which everybody would understand. But I think it is a question of your immediate audience. In most cases when I start writing, I feel I am writing for the Tanzanian audience first and foremost, because I am dealing with problems which are relevant to the Tanzanian audience. So it is only after the writing that I could think of the audience beyond the borders of Tanzania.

Adeola: In an interview which you gave in 1974, you did say you would consider translating your plays into English. Has any of them been translated yet?

Penina: Unfortunately not, I have never gotten round to doing it. I don't know why, but I'd rather work on a new play than translate those that are already published.

Adeola: To the wider African literary public your work presents the problem of distribution, the problem of language as well as that of criticism. For example, even though you have been publishing plays

75

since 1972, your works were not familiar to most people at that conference which I referred to. For that reason, it was really difficult to
judge whether the evaluation and interpretation of the plays was
valid or not. What is your opinion on these problems? Do you expect
your plays to be judged only by people who can read Swahili?

Penina: Well, I think that problem is very deep. The reasons why
writers in Africa, generally, don't get known has many angles. We
know who has the power to distribute the materials, and they have
the choice as to what material they want to distribute. For instance,
many writers have come up in Africa, even among women; but you
only see a few names such as Soyinka, Ngugi, Achebe and so on.
These are the writers of the sixties, but we are in the eighties now. I
think then, that, in a way, those who have the power to distribute
continue to use their own criteria for promoting the people they want
for their own purposes. And taking into account the problems we
have in Africa in terms of exchange of material and of communi-
cating; you know how long it takes a letter from Tanzania to get to
Nigeria? These are problems that are beyond our control and I think
these are the major problems.

Adeola: Of course, when Kiswahili becomes the official language for
the whole of Africa the problem of communication will be mini-
mized. Do you think this ideal of a common continental language
will ever be realised?

Penina: Looking at the problems that Africa is having – the disunity
economically, politically, ideologically – I am becoming a bit disillusioned about the possibility of a continental language. But I don't
want to be pessimistic, I really hope that it happens, though it might
even take five or six decades from now to materialize. Things are not
changing for the better.

Adeola: Have you attended any African writers' conference? How do
you relate to other writers?

Penina: This is an interesting question. Maybe for the reasons you
pointed out earlier, I have never been invited to any African writers'
conference. One time I was in Zimbabwe and there was a conference
on African writers going on. I was really surprised that I didn't even
know about it previously. But as I said earlier, it is always the
Achebes and the Soyinkas and the Ngugis who get invited because
the organizers of such conferences have certain interests.

Adeola: Some of your plays, such as *Hatia* ('Guilt'), *Pambo*
('Decoration'), *Nguzo-Mama* ('Mother-Pillar') and *Talaka si
Mke Wangu* ('Woman, I Divorce You'), focus on the problems of
women. We are told that the views reflected in these plays are that
women are disunited, that though they are aware of their individual
problems they have failed to forge unity amongst themselves, that
they are intellectually and morally confused. Obviously, you are
concerned about the problems of women, so how have your plays

been received in Tanzania, the society out of which you write?

Penina: I must say that the reception of my plays has been better than I expected. The common audience for my work seems to appreciate most of them. But I haven't created so much debate around the woman issue. A lot of debate has come out on my plays generally; but not specifically on the woman issue. I don't know whether it is because, as women, we haven't made a deliberate attempt to discuss the women's issues that come out in the plays. Many women have given me comments, but only in passing. For example, women have made interesting comments on *Nguzo Mama*; however, not critical material like what happens in the university classroom. So I can't really assess the impact of the plays from that angle.

Adeola: In the interview that I referred to earlier you said, 'I strongly believe that in Tanzania we can't afford to have art for art's sake . . . because we have got so many problems as a developing country and . . . because the artist has got such a big task to help in this development'. Your plays, such as *Tambueni Haki Zetu* ('Recognize Our Rights') and *Harakari za Ukombozi* ('Liberation Struggles'), address specific contemporary African problems. Have you noticed the impact of these plays on the problems in any way, I mean the problems of liberation and those of human rights?

Penina: Well, again it is difficult to assess the impact. We did a production of *Harakari za Ukombozi* and it generated a lot of debate because it was a critical assessment of the history of struggle in this country, from the pre-colonial period to the period of *Ujamaa* (socialist) policies. It created quite a lot of debate. People liked the production very much. The other one which may have been even more controversial is *Lena Ubani*, which was produced last year. It dealt with the major political problems of Tanzania between 1982–85. It was an assessment of the economic situation and the way things were going. That created much more debate than I expected. So if we are talking about impact in terms of the reaction of the audience, my plays have been received here in a way that is beyond my expectations; which is quite satisfying to a writer.

Adeola: You say that you write for the common man in Tanzania. That seems to me to be quite vague. Does it mean that you deal only with the problems of the common man? Can a univeristy audience be entertained by your plays?

Penina: I have been trying to write in a way that is relevant to and addresses a general audience. I have done deliberate experiments, especially with the form. I have done some research into African traditional theatre forms. So I have been using the Tanzanian traditional forms like songs and storytelling, dance and recitation, so as to come up with plays which will appeal to the Tanzanian cultural identity.

But I have also been trying to make my plays simple enough to be understood by any Tanzanian, from any walk of life, including the university students. The last production was particularly interesting to me because it was discussing some very topical political issues and I was really interested to gauge how the audience from different walks of life would react to it. I remember there was one man who came to see the play from a very remote village in Mwanza. He was brought to see the play by a relative. He enjoyed this play so much. When we discussed it, he was saying how close the problems depicted in the play were to the problems which they were going through. He commented, 'So you do know about our problems, why are you not taking any action about them?' That was very touching for me. He was discussing it at the same level as the university audience that was present.

Adeola: The play is called *Lena Ubani*. What does it mean?

Penina: It means 'there is an anti-dote for rot'. It is a reversal of the Swahili proverb which says there is no anti-dote for rot.

Adeola: That sounds fantastic. Well, I hope the people, after seeing your play, believe that there is an anti-dote for all social ills and begin to act more positively.

Penina: I hope so, because the main argument of the play is that sometimes when the nation goes through all these problems we tend to come up with reasons – 'It is because of this, because of that' – and then things get worse and worse and worse. What I am arguing is that, that kind of trend can be stopped so that the society can change for the better.

Adeola: *Recognize our Rights* and *Liberation Struggles* are overtly political. In fact, after listening to you, it would appear that all your plays are political. It is also clear from your previous statements that people appreciate your message and you are pleased with their reception. Where have your plays been performed?

Penina: *Recognize our Rights* has been performed mostly in the schools. *Liberation Struggles* has been performed in Dar-es-Salaam, in Zanzibaar; also in schools because most of my books are on the reading list for schools.

Adeola: Have there been public performances apart from those in the schools?

Penina: Yes.

Adeola: On the whole, are you pleased with the reception of all the plays?

Penina: I will say 'yes'. The only problem is that we don't get the opportunity to have as many performances as we would wish because we don't have professional theatre along western lines. It is difficult, for instance, to run a production for three to four months. The general situation in Tanzania is that you work hard on a production and it is performed publicly for only five or six, or at the most, ten shows. This is not enough, one wishes whatever company is performing could do a lot of shows all over the country; but it is not easy.

Adeola: Is there a drama company as such?

Penina: We do have amateur groups, not a company that is based in a particular place, having their own theatre house. No. But we have amateur groups that perform in different places like community centres.

Adeola: I think this is true throughout Africa at the moment except in Nigeria where a few professional theatre groups have emerged. African critics have commented that the novel form is alien to the Africans whilst drama is the most natural seeing that most of our rituals and entertainments are dramatic performances. Have you managed to combine both the traditional form of entertainment with the requirements of the modern theatre in your plays?

Penina: In fact, that has been my major preoccupation. Because of my interest in traditional African theatre, sometimes I wonder if my plays are plays at all. I think I have disregarded the conventions of what would be regarded as a good play from the western point of view. I am much more interested in experimentations with different African traditional forms. The latter half of my plays are really something else; not plays as you would expect but a mixture of various forms, such as storytelling, dance and recitation. Sometimes I pick up digests, expressions which are not necessarily a complete dramatic form in the traditional context. For example, the way people sing at a funeral or at a traditional religious ritual. Sometimes, I select heroic recitations or dances. I've mostly been interested in the art of storytelling to see how I can combine that with the dramatic art. So most of my plays are around that kind of experimentation.

Adeola: Are you quite pleased with the results that are coming out?

Penina: Yes. What I am doing, I must say, is not in isolation. This department (Department of Theatre Arts at the University of Dar-es-Salaam) has actually embarked on a deliberate approach to develop the Tanzanian traditional theatre forms. So a lot of the work which is being done in the department is geared towards that kind of experimentation. My writing is part of that general change of orientation.

Adeola: What strikes me as you describe the general principles guiding your theatrical productions is that there are other people doing the type of things you are doing. There is a Jamaican, Trevor Rhone, who in his play *Old Story Time*, makes use of the setting of a traditional storytelling performance.

To what extent have the revolutionary changes that were ushered in by the Arusha Declaration and Education for Self Reliance shaped your stance as a writer?

Penina: I must say that it has been very fertile. I mean, the coming of the 'Arusha Declaration' and the adoption of *Ujamaa* have in general created very fertile ground for artistic creation in this country. But in my work, personally, I think it has triggered my imagination. Especially, to look at the changes which the society has been going through because of the *Ujamaa* policies and all the efforts to construct a socialist society. There have been enormous things happening in this country that are really so exciting for an artist. The changes that have taken place have affected the lives of the people in so many different ways.

But I must say, as I look at my work, I think I have changed with the years. At first, I was very much obsessed with the whole ideal of *Ujamaa* and I think this can be detected in my earlier works. This was a stage which every Tanzanian went through, creating this ideal society where everybody would be equal, where there would be no exploitation, where you are going to school, not because of yourself, but because you need to serve the society. I mean, the ideals of *Ujamaa* were attractive to everybody. And then later on, we all realized that building *Ujamaa* is not all that easy, when we started seeing the problems, when things started going wrong. Some of these problems were not coming out in public, but a lot of things were going wrong. At the same time, it also became interesting for the writer to find out what it was that was going wrong. In the latter part of my writing I think I really show my disillusionment with the way some sectors of the society have taken advantage of the problems of building *Ujamaa*, actually almost turning the whole experiment to their own advantage. I think my later works show that disillusionment with a dream that has gone foul.

Adeola: Do you usually have an audience comprising of different sectors of the society?

Penina: Yes.

Adeola: Those whom the shoe fits, so to speak, how do they react to your plays?

Penina: That is something which is very interesting about Tanzania. People feel that because we are building socialism there is a lot of repression in terms of the freedom of expression. But in my work, people have seen the performances, even top officials of the government. I have been through experiences where people have come to me and said, 'You are now tired of your children. Why do you want to say these things and go to jail?' But people have come to see the plays from all walks of life. Well, of course, they don't all agree with what I say. Definitely not. But I think they have all discussed the works. This is especially true of the last play.

Adeola: Are you referring to *There is Remedy for Rot*?

Penina: Yes. In fact, it generated so much debate that the central executive of the national ruling party requested to see it. So we had to have a special show for the Party, the Central Committee and the National Executive Committee. We didn't understand why they wanted to see it. Of course, there was a lot of debate, people were saying things like 'now you are being accommodated', and so on. But the high officials saw and discussed the play and one got the impression that they felt that it was important for them to know what the people were thinking even if it was not in their favour.

Adeola: Well, here is literature fulfilling its practical function within society – making people think and making the rulers aware of what the populace thinks about them.

Penina: It was quite interesting. It showed that, maybe, there is much more freedom of expression than people had thought. Not that the Government or the Party likes the criticism but there is much more political maturity in listening to what people say even if you do not take any action about it, even if you just ignore it afterwards. Since then, that was about two years ago, many more Tanzanians are coming out and looking at, and saying things much more critically than used to be the case, five or six years back. To what effect, I don't know. But I think it is an interesting development.

Adeola: You have published nine plays and a collection of African Tales within a period of 14 years. How has your art evolved during this period? Have you noticed, for example, any development in terms of theme, craft and perspective?

Penina: I suppose it is the critics who can answer such a question fully. However, when you look at your own work, you do see a kind of growth. I mean like when I read my earlier plays, I can see the difference in the way I treat a theme. I used to do it in a more simplistic manner than I do today. I think you grow up, in the sense of going for the more complicated theme, or maybe themes that are much more deep, as you go on writing. Whereas, in my earlier plays I would develop the theme only in relation to the story line, as in the story of *Hatia*, the girl who goes into the town and then gets into trouble, now, I follow the story much more by looking into the problem of why that girl went to town, why she had to go back to the village, what were the forces that made her behave that way. When I look at my later plays I see myself looking at the broader social issues, so that the character is more developed. I suppose this development in a writer parallels the growth of a person according to her age or her experience.

Adeola: Would you describe your writing process?

Penina: Oh! It is chaotic (laughs). I am a very unpredictable person. I don't write according to any plan. Normally what happens, I can go for one or two or even three years without writing. Then something will start nagging me about certain problem. Without even making a decision to write, I just start following the different angles. Then I start getting excited about certain themes, then I will do a little research into that particular theme. But it comes sort of vaguely and I normally spend quite some time putting information together on how I should expand that theme and from what different angles.

Then the characters start coming, and I start formulating different events before I get down to writing. Normally, when I start writing I can do it quickly. When that happens I put away other things. I will spend about a whole month just writing until I finish. And I have to finish it.

Adeola: Before you can breathe again.

Penina: Yes. And then after I've finished the first draft, then I can go and sort of polish it, like reworking the dialogue and some of the characters. This doesn't bother me, what is important is that the whole thing must be on paper.

Adeola: It takes you a whole month to write a play? What about your teaching?

Penina: Normally, I will do that. But I do just the basic, if there are other things like writing papers for a conference, I put them aside. So I spend all the spare time concentrating on writing the play.

Adeola: As a committed writer, it would appear that you see your most important preoccupation as the development of Swahili literature. Is that a correct assessment?

Penina: I always say that writing in Kiswahili is for me automatic. I cannot see myself writing in English. I do feel at home writing in a language which I feel I have mastered much better than any other. So that even the urge to write in English really doesn't come. Sometimes when I write, I almost feel like writing in my mother tongue; there are some expressions which come so beautifully in the mother tongue. But there is also the question of developing Swahili literature, which is also very important, because we are lucky in Tanzania to have this one language. So I think it is only natural that the writing be done in Kiswahili, which is adding to the richness of the language. Even in my life time, Kiswahili has gained momentum, it is growing up as a language. Some new terms are coming up, new expressions. Even when you are writing you find you are using different tenses that you wouldn't have used five or six years ago. The language itself is growing very, very fast.

Adeola: Do you agree with the opinion that African women writers should be responsible first and foremost to women?

Penina: I wouldn't say 'first and foremost'. Maybe some feminists will call this a backward stance. I do argue very strongly that the woman issue cannot be separated from the overall problems, since women cannot be separated from the rest of the society. I believe that the liberation of the woman has to be part of the liberation of the society itself. First and foremost, the society has to understand that it has got to be liberated; that every problem that affects the woman also affects the society at large.

In my plays, I like to present something which is relevant to both men and women, even if it is specifically a woman issue. But a man should understand what the problem is because he also has an important part to play. If you just addressed the women, that would be unsatisfactory because the problem would only be half–solved. I wouldn't put it 'first and foremost' in terms of who I should address. But I will agree with that statement in terms of taking as many opportunities as possible to bring out the issues that affect women because if we don't do it, the men are not going to do it for us. Definitely, the woman writer has a responsibility to work for women. I agree with the statement from that point of view, but not in isolation.

Adeola: A critic, Molara Ogundipe-Leslie said that the female writer should be committed in three ways: as a writer, as a woman and a Third World person. What is your opinion on this statement?

Penina: I think it is true. The issues that you bring out as a writer indicate that you recognize your responsibility towards the society at large. But I don't think there is any topic you can write about where the women do not feature. I was given an example in one workshop. I have been very much involved in the popular theatre movement, where we go and work in the village. We use theatre as a means through which people can discuss and analyse their problems, put them into a theatrical performance, show it to the audience and then discuss what the solutions should be. When we first started working on the popular theatre movement, we did not design it deliberately to engage 'the women issue' as such. But as soon as we started working, the women issue always came up in whichever problem we dealt with at the village level.

Adeola: Were the people you were dealing with mostly women?

Penina: No, everybody, all the members of the village, men, women and children. Yet, in spite of that, the women issue always dominated. It showed me in a very practical way that the women issue is so central to every aspect of life that no writer can afford to ignore it. And I think the woman writer has that responsibility as a woman to highlight the issues. And of course, when you are writing about Third World issues, you are writing about the problems of Africa, the problems of Tanzania, which must be looked at from a Third World perspective.

Adeola: Writing in a revolutionary environment, as a woman writer, do you encounter the backward attitude that a woman's place is in the home? Or are you taken seriously as a writer and an academic?

Penina: I think, on home ground, I have enjoyed a lot of support. I really can't cite an incident where I was slighted or I couldn't write or couldn't publish because I am a woman. This is something which I am saying very frankly. On home ground, I have received a lot of support, yet there are male writers around. The kind of support I am getting from my audience has never made me feel that I am less capable because I am a woman. In fact, in most cases, I feel that I am enjoying much more support than I deserve.

Adeola: What about your colleagues?

Penina: With my colleagues I enjoy very good working relations. When my works are being discussed my colleagues discuss them as any other works, not necessarily as a woman's works. But I wouldn't say the same thing for the international gathering. There, I feel the woman writer is really being ignored. Like that conference in Zimbabwe that I referred to earlier, there was only one woman writer present. And it was supposed to have been an African writers' workshop. So I think on the broader field there is a problem.

Adeola: When did you know you were a writer?

Penina: I don't know if I even know it now. Perhaps there is a hypocrite telling me that I am a writer.

Adeola: After publishing so many plays, why should you not enjoy the feeling of knowing that you are a writer?

Penina: It always challenges you when people refer to you as a writer. Then you ask yourself, 'Oh! am I really doing the things which a writer is supposed to do?' I have always been interested in writing, it is something that has been with me for a long time. I started writing even when I was in the primary school. We used to have these small drama groups where you were supposed to come up with your own play for Parents' Day. I remember I used to write short scripts; I don't know if they made sense but I have been interested in writing since then. I can't say when I really began to get the feeling of being a writer. Maybe the first thing that brought this to mind was when my first play was accepted for publication. I was completely unprepared because I had written that play as part of my undergraduate assignments. Then my lecturer liked it and he sent it to a publisher, who said it was a good play and he would publish it. This came as a complete surprise.

Adeola: That was *Hatia*.

Penina: No, it was another one – *Heshima Yangu* (My Respects). *Hatia* was the first one to be published but it was not my first play. *Heshima Yangu* was a very short play. Maybe the publication of that play brought the realization that I could go on and write.

Adeola: Is writing now a way of life for you or do you find fulfilment in other areas of life?

Penina: I think writing has to go with other things. I am saying this because I have been quite dissatisfied with writing alone. I have felt that writing alone does not have an immediate impact. Especially writing in the dramatic form, where you have to wait for someone to take the play and produce it, then you wait for how many people will come and see the show. Here in Tanzania, sometimes, it takes a long time before a written play is produced at all. I have felt more dissatisfied because the plays are not quite effective with the peasants because they never get the chance to see them. When we are talking of the theatre as a means for development, then we cannot restrict it to the urban areas where the plays are performed. That is why I got actively involved in this Popular Theatre Movement or what is called Theatre for Development, because then you get into a community in the rural areas. For instance, even in the urban areas, you can use theatre as part of the developmental process. The people become involved and they use their own skills of singing, dancing and storytelling to discuss the developmental problems which they are facing, and they come out with a solution. In that process writing is irrelevant, because the people are making the theatre themselves.

Adeola: You mean they move away from your play or you concentrate on seeing what is coming out from them?

Penina: We don't take any play to them. What we do is just go there and spend some time. We stay in the village and do research, know what are their problems in that area.

Adeola: You go as a theatre group – staff and students?

Penina: Yes.

Adeola: How does that produce a play?

Penina: After you have done the research with them, then you sit down together with different people and discuss the problems. Then you improvise, to put the research material into a theatrical form. You have to use a theatrical form familiar to the people, dance drama, dramatic skit or storytelling, whatever. But everybody is involved in the creative process. Nobody writes a script because the play is being created as you perform it.

Adeola: How long do you spend in the village?

Penina: Normally not less than two weeks. We usually go during the vacation. It became such an exciting experience that I realised that writing was not important in that kind of experience. Writing becomes important only as a documentation of what happened. By then the theatrical experience has taken place. I think it is enriching, because when you come back to the ordinary writing of plays, it has given you a very practical experience of what people feel in that community. So it sort of broadens your ideas. That gave me the realisation that it is not enough to be a writer. There is so much in the practical field that can be done, even without writing.

Adeola: Do you think writers are different from other people?

Penina: Oh no, I wouldn't say that. They are very ordinary. I always get embarrassed the way people react when they see me, because a writer is a very ordinary person, there is nothing unusual about her.

Adeola: You must realise that other people feel differently. But how you feel is a reflection of the philosophy of your society. I presume that here a writer is a worker like anybody else. In your role as a writer you are helping to demystify some of the barriers of class associated with certain professions. You certainly reflect the attitude of the Tanzanian society where nobody tries to put on any airs; whatever you do, you are making a contribution and you are appreciated for it, whether you are a writer, a labourer or a farmer.

Penina: Exactly.

Adeola: Why are there so few African women writers? Why is it we have not yet produced a writer of the stature of Achebe, Ngugi and Soyinka?

Penina: I think we have to look at this question in a very positive way. I think there are very good women artists. If you look at the traditional performances the women are some of the best performers. But when it comes to writing it is the men who are given prominence. If you look at the village, who are the best storytellers? It is the women. Who are the dancers? It is the women. So I think that, on the one hand, there is a deliberate attempt not to give prominence to women writers. I don't think this trend is confined to Africa alone, because I think this happened in Europe in the past. In many cases, men do not like challenges from women. So I suppose it is understandable when there is a writers' conference that men can only think of other male writers as being their equals or worthy of coming to the same table and discussing their works. As a writer, very few men writers are interested in my work. Even when you meet them they hardly feel that they need to discuss your work. I feel it is part of the man/woman problem that you find in other sectors.

On the other hand, I think we have to look at it from a broader perspective. The women have suffered historically, being left behind even when they are very capable, because of the structure of the society. Very good performers and dancers exist in the village, but when it comes to writing it is the men who have gone to school, where they learned to write. The men have had a better chance than the women to develop their talent. In the area of drama, it is even more serious because many people still feel that women should not be performers. It is seen as a profession which is despised, therefore respectable women should not be performing on the stage. This is a big contradiction because in a society like Tanzania, if you go to the village, our mothers are the dancers and the storytellers. Why is it that when you come to the city and a woman stands on the stage performing she becomes cheap? There are all these contradictions which really don't make sense and they have all contributed towards making the woman writer remain unrecognized compared to the man.

Adeola: Do you see any differences in the ways African male and female writers handle theme, character and situation?

Penina: I haven't studied that, so I cannot answer that question comprehensively. But I have a general feeling that men writers are much more careless when it comes to portraying women. I feel that what they do reflects their behaviour towards the women in their own lives. I am not saying, however, that all the women writers are conscious or that they write about women more positively. But I think the negative orientation of the male writer comes out much more clearly.

Adeola: There are only a few African women writers, and women dramatists like yourself are fewer still. A female critic suggested that this
might be because the husbands cannot put up with the demands of
the long hours required for producing plays. How have you managed to cope with the demands of being an academic, a dramatist and
a home maker?

Penina: I must say it is not easy and I always disagree with women
who answer that kind of question by saying that they have a way of
balancing, that they manage. I would like to find out the formula. I
think in one way or another something has to suffer. For instance, in
my work, between my academic responsibility, my writing and my
children to be able to pay equal attention to all of them, I have to
work extra hard, day and night. If I don't have the ability to do that
then one of them has to suffer. I'll have to spend more time at the
office and not see the family at all, or else spend time with the family
and leave something pending at the office. So I always say that it is
not easy. I am not saying that it is not manageable because we have
managed; many women have managed.

As far as my husband is concerned, he has been very supportive
and I have not had any kind of problem. With my type of work – not
only am I in the theatre but I am also involved in administration,
being a head of department, and with the teaching, sometimes I
spend hours and hours away from home. I also travel a lot. I have to
spend long rehearsing hours during production. But he has been very
supportive. I have been very fortunate from that aspect, otherwise
there would have been a lot of problems.

Adeola: How does your family like the idea of your being a writer?

Penina: This is an interesting question. My daughter doesn't like it at
all. She came to me one day and asked, 'Why did you become a
writer?' I tried to find out why she asked the question, and she
explained that she didn't like the idea of people coming to her all the
time and saying, 'This is Penina's daughter'. Why can't they say,
'This is Muta', she protested.

Adeola: At present it appears as if you are eclipsing her own personality, but hopefully some day she will understand and she will be
proud of her mother.

Now to my next question. Would it give greater weight to the collective voice of women in Africa if the writers were to foster a union,
a communication link, amongst themselves?

Penina: I am not aware of any union and, as a matter of fact, I am not
in touch with other African women writers, unfortunately. I have
tried and others have also tried but the problem of communication
has made contact between ourselves very, very minimal. I always
feel bad that I don't know what these people are doing because I am
sure there is a lot that we can learn from one another. I would say
there is a lot to gain through that kind of union. I am saying this

because in 1983 we formed a Union of African Performing Artists, and within three years it is fantastic the kind of contacts which we have made just by having a union. Today, I know that if I want something in the area of the performing arts in certain countries I know who to contact. So the idea of a union has a lot of advantages because it brings you together. If this could be achieved among the women writers it would be very useful.

Adeola: Is there a black or African aesthetic? If so, how is this reflected in your writings? It is an old question and maybe it has out-lived its usefulness.

Penina: Oh! no. It is still very relevant, especially in the area of the performing arts. Much work has been done in African theatre, but you can see in the practice of theatre, the way people still cling to the European conventions, and try to write like Europeans. Even in 1986, people are still doing foreign plays! There is definitely an African aesthetic, which has been down-played because of our colonial history. There are certain elements of the African traditional performance which can best be understood and enjoyed by an African audience. These are the things we need to bring out and see how they can best serve the expectations of a contemporary audience. This will revolutionize the theatrical arts, combining them with what we know of the European conventional theatre. There is still much more to be done with the African tradition. To give this simple example, I have noticed the way the African audience laughs, even when the play is tragic. The point is, that Africans are not callous people, it doesn't mean they enjoy seeing people murdered, it means they have a different perception. Maybe they are laughing at the perfection of the acting, seeing that the actor has managed to imitate the action so well. I don't know, but these are things that need to be researched.

Adeola: What impact has the women's movement had on you as an African woman writer?

Penina: Quite a lot. I must say that I wasn't aware of the woman issue when I started writing, but with the years I have understood the woman issue much better, and I am conscious now of those issues particularly relating to women, when I am writing, or even when I am acting or doing the experimental work that I spoke about earlier. Once you feel that women should not be portrayed in a certain way, you become very sensitive when somebody portrays them wrongly. It has been very helpful, even in my own growing as a woman and in my understanding of the position of the woman in society.

Adeola: Can an African woman make a living from writing alone? Would you like to be in that position?

Penina: From my experience it is almost impossible to make a living by writing. Speaking from the Tanzanian situation, writing is not profitable. First of all, the readership is very limited, maybe because we write in Kiswahili. In Africa, widespread illiteracy is a constraint on readership. Then, generally speaking, Africans have not cultivated the habit of reading. We are an oral people.

I would love to see the day when I would have a lot of time to think and to create. My administrative responsibility takes up a lot of my time, rushing to this meeting and that meeting. By the end of the day you are so tired that you can hardly think. So it is very distracting to do all those other things which one needs to do to earn a reasonable living. One wishes one could find time just to sit and write.

Adeola: Are there other barriers, either inward or outward, personal or social, that you have had to grapple with as a writer?

Penina: My main problem is finding adequate time. It is very frustrating, though I don't know how to solve that particular problem. I have also had problems with publishing, mainly because the publishing industry in this country is still undeveloped. Right now I am not the only writer having problems with the publishers – everybody is. Of course, it is much more difficult to publish outside Tanzania. Firstly, because the works are in Kiswahili; secondly, it is difficult to handle the legal aspects, such as copyright and distribution. This has been very frustrating. For example, you send a work to a publisher outside and they like it. But it takes them six years to get it out. So by the time they publish the book, it is out of date.

The other problem is that my work has not gone on the stage as fast as I would want. It is really not satisfactory to publish a play before it is performed, it doesn't give you a chance to see how it works. If it is performed after it has been published, you may want to change certain things because they don't work practically; but it is too late.

Adeola: Can African women writers help to resolve some of the debates concerning our underdevelopment and the oppression of women by men?

Penina: This is an area that is rightly gaining prominence now, because this is a forum that is accessible to women and they must use it as much as possible. In the struggle for women's liberation we have to use all the means at our disposal. Writing is a very effective tool and it should be used for that purpose. That was why I was very pleased by the NGO section (Non Governmental Organisations) at the celebration of the Decade of Women, when they gave prominence to art, and the role of artistic works in the whole question of women. They organized poetry readings and theatre performances, and some people read excerpts from their novels. There was a realization that artistic activities are an integral part of the struggle for women's liberation.

Adeola: Does being a woman constitute any definite advantage or disadvantage for you as a writer?

Penina: During the actual writing I have faced certain frustrations. Particularly dealing with drama, when, to a certain extent, you try to portray reality, and when you are creating the characters, you try to place them in their settings. This creates a conflict for the writer when she comes to women characters. You want them to be positive, but sometimes the situation can be so bad that you have to portray them as they are. For instance, this question of having a negative female character such as a prostitute. If a play calls for the presentation of a prostitute, you still feel that it is not positive to cast women in such a negative role. Yet you have to portray the reality in the society in order to present your message. At the same time, you are aware of the contradiction, the conflict, of wanting the positive aspect of women to come out, and not to compromise reality. I find this very problematic. I don't know if a novelist feels the same problem but it is a problem that preoccupies the dramatist, for whom the credibility of a character within the social reality is a very pressing issue. Maybe that is one of the disadvantages of being a woman writer. Perhaps a male writer doesn't spend much time agonizing over how he portrays his female characters.

Adeola: Your plays deal with contemporary and immediate problems facing Tanzania. How do you create timelessness and universality then?

Penina: In terms of timelessness, I don't know whether what I talk about are the kinds of things that will stand the test of time, I'm not sure I can evaluate that. In terms of the universality, I believe most of the problems relating to Tanzania are relative to other places, especially other African countries.

Adeola: Writing in a society that is conscious of its commitment to socialist ideology, does your writing have an ideological base?

Penina: I hope so. I hope the ideology is socialism. Yes, that is what I think I am portraying, but it is the works themselves which will tell how successful I have been.

Adeola: Is the transition between creating the work and directing it a challenging encounter?

Penina: Unfortunately, I haven't directed one of my own plays yet. I hesitate to direct because I am not very good at it. Secondly, it is much better to get someone else to interpret afresh, to try out things which you yourself cannot see because you have one fixed idea. I have strictly left my works to others and I enjoy seeing others interpret my works.

Adeola: Are there other female writers in Tanzania?

Penina: Yes, Amandina Liharba is a playwright. She wrote an adaptation of Sembene Ousmane's *The Money-Order* and she co-authored *Harakati* ('Liberation Struggles') with me.

Adeola: What would be your advice to prospective female writers in the light of your own experience?

Penina: Whoever wants to write should just go ahead and do it because they can do it. Try it and do not hesitate. With many women there is this lack of confidence. Many women bring things for me to read. When I say they are good and they must go ahead, they say, 'I can't, I am just trying this out'. In the women's organizations that I am involved in, we are trying to instil this confidence into women.

Adeola: Writing in Kiswahili, do you feel you are working in isolation, or do you borrow from the great tradition of Swahili writers like Shaaban Roberts, and Mwalimu Nyerere's translations of *Julius Caesar* and *The Merchant of Venice*, which I understand are so good that they are like original plays?

Penina: The works of Shaaban Roberts and Mwalimu are unparalleled, but these are not works that I have followed or imitated. This is mainly because their Kiswahili is so good that I cannot follow their tradition. They are people whose works I enjoy reading because they are very good.

Adeola: Would you say that they wrote in classical Kiswahili?

Penina: Yes, it is not Kiswahili for a common readership, it is for people who are highly educated, or people along the coast.

Adeola: Are your plays studied in schools and universities?

Penina: Yes, throughout Tanzania. They are part of Swahili literature in schools and colleges of art. Actually the schools represent the biggest readership of my works.

Adeola: Have you tried writing in another medium besides drama?

Penina: I've tried, but for some reason I can't. I've tried to write a novel, but find that expressing myself in the dramatic form is more effective.

Adeola: Finally, Okot p'Bitek, the renowned Ugandan poet, (who wrote *Song of Lawino* in Acholi and then himself translated it into English) pointed out that, 'Economics and politics are the most important factors affecting the development of vernacular literature'. How have these two factors affected your writing?

Penina: In terms of politics, the Tanzanian policy on language is very positive. This has been contributory to my growth as a writer. I don't have to go through the problem that a writer writing in Uganda or Kenya will go through, of being accused of using a tribal language. About economics, I agree from the point of view that writers who write in Kiswahili have a very limited audience and so cannot make money. I am not sure that the same is true of those writing in English or French or Portuguese. I would like to find out whether these writers are making more money than those few writing in the vernacular. Especially since most people are not literate and most of our people are still struggling to buy food; buying a book, for them, is quite a luxury. Maybe if one writes in English or French, having a European audience is useful. But this is not manifest to me; when I travel abroad I've been very frustrated about how little people know about Africa.

Micere Mugo

Micere Githae Mugo is Kenyan by birth. She studied at the University of Makerere in Uganda and later earned a doctorate degree from the University of Toronto in Canada. She is a Marxist, concerned with the fate of Africa since Independence, who uses her writing as a revolutionary weapon. Inevitably she became involved in the revolutionary process in Kenya whilst she was a senior lecturer and Dean of the Faculty of Arts at the University of Nairobi. Like Ngugi wa Thiong'o, a close colleague of hers, she has been exiled from her homeland since 1982 for political reasons. Living in Zimbabwe, however, she does not consider herself an exile, as the struggle there is part of the same struggle that embraces the whole of Africa. She has been teaching at the University of Zimbabwe since 1982.

Her publications include a collection of poetry, *Daughter of My People, Sing!* (1976); two plays, *The Long Illness of Ex-Chief Kiti* (1976) and jointly with Ngugi wa Thiong'o *The Trial of Dedan Kimathi* (1976); and a book of criticism, *Visions of Africa* (1981).

9

Micere Githae Mugo

This interview was conducted at the University of Zimbabwe, Harare, 12 July 1986.

Adeola: Would you like to summarise the radical changes that have taken place in your life in these past three or four years?

Micere: It will be very difficult to pin down the many things that have happened to me during the last three or four years. I think the only thing that I can possibly say is that I have grown a lot in terms of ideological orientation, and my complete commitment to the transition of our African societies, and the so-called Third World, from capitalism to socialism. For one major reason: that we are dealing with a philosophy that agrees that it is wrong for just a few to possess when the majority are dispossessed.

What led to my leaving Kenya has to do with the responsibility that I held as Dean of the biggest faculty at the University of Nairobi, the Faculty of Arts, the things that I said, and the confidence colleagues and students had in me, in electing me to such an important position. Can one compromise and act as if one is betraying these very people who have voted one into the position of authority and trust, by acting as if one is a policewoman towards them? Academically and intellectually, they have no freedom, whatever they say is censored. It is very difficult, in Kenyan society, to speak one's mind, especially if one takes a position that is pro-socialism. One faces harrassment and imprisonment.

I felt, therefore, that with my obvious commitment to this kind of development, it was going to be of no use to find myself behind bars or to have to compromise my position, not being able to speak my mind or write what I think. So I have opted to live outside my country. So long as I live on the African continent, I can carry on the struggle which, essentially, is the same.

Adeola: Is it inevitable for the artist who speaks to her people to have to leave her home environment?

Micere: I don't think it is inevitable, but not to can be quite tricky. The task of the artist, and, indeed, of any of us, who seeks a change that will better the lives of our people, is actually to stay at home and struggle with the people there in order to bring about this change. But I feel that it is adventurist, a way of wanting to be a martyr, which doesn't help anybody, to see a situation in which an artist or teacher, whatever, is obviously going to end up behind bars, and continue to wait for it to happen. I think it is better to go and use your talent somewhere else. The artist has a choice. The one who has decided to speak for her people, the oppressed, and to take sides with them, has got a very, very difficult line of existence indeed, whether one is living at home or outside, because the struggle continues even when one is outside.

As I said earlier, mine was a very conscious choice. I had enough evidence to know that it was going to be very difficult for me to live outside and live free unless I were to shut up and I have a problem with shutting up. When I really believe in something I want to say it. I don't want to compromise. I took this as maybe another tactic that writers and revolutionaries have to learn – to shut their mouths and keep quiet at critical moments, as a strategy.

Adeola: Do you think that in Africa, your type of experience has compromised many writers or has even prevented others from becoming writers?

Micere: What I do know is that if you really have the urge to be a writer, it is very difficult for anything to stop you. Having said that, I must admit that there is a lot of talent among people who cannot read and write today, but of course they cannot sit down and write. Some of them compose and produce in form of orature. So I make the previous statement and then take it back. What I mean by saying that if you have the urge to write nothing can stop you, is that if you do have the facilities and the ability and the skill to write, I think it is very difficult for any one to stop you. As many of us have seen, you lock a man or a woman up in prison and they find a way of collecting bits and pieces and they continue writing. They learn to train their memory to retain a lot of the things that they are composing and later on they put it on paper. It is really not a very difficult thing since you have the images that you are writing about gazing at you full in the face.

Adeola: Do you ever wish that you were not charged with this agonizing responsibility to write?

Micere: It keeps happening to me. I have many things in my mind that I want to write about, many manuscripts that I have started and have not been able to complete. So that I get frustrated, and at such moments I sort of wish I did not have the urge to write. Sometimes, I cannot go to sleep because of this frustration. However, a new kind of person is emerging who is so deeply involved in community affairs and happenings within where I am living that, much as I want to get away from it, I am not successful. I find myself at schools speaking to school children, at colleges in Harare and other places. There is so much to be done that I tell myself, 'Well, you cannot say no to any of these calls because Africa is in a crisis. You don't know what may happen tomorrow. So long as you are doing these things you are, as it were, writing a poem that will never find itself on the pages of a book, but at least it may have touched another person's soul'.

Adeola: Do you think writers are different from other people?

Micere: I want to insist very firmly that writers are not different from other people. They are very ordinary people, like the people in the villages, in the factories, out there, wherever people are. The only advantage, talking about the writer who actually communicates through putting pen to paper – most of us are spoilt brats – is that we have good jobs, good houses, places where we can actually write. We are spoilt because of this image of a writer as an exceptional person, to be treated exceptionally and so on. I want to repeat what Okelo Oculi said at a writers' conference, I think it was in Washington D.C. He said, 'In Africa writers cannot afford the luxury of acting like spoilt children. We are ordinary people. Any writer who is not recognized in her or his village by the villagers and ordinary people is not worthy of being called a writer'.

Having said that, I do want to add that a writer has a special talent in that not everybody . . . can actually write. I think you have to have that gift of originality, in terms of being able to give an extra dimension to the world you perceive; in terms of being able to be moved by images, by incidents, by people in such a way that you want to comment about them. Writing is a creative process, therefore I feel that writers should be concerned with the destructive elements and political systems which impede and arrest our people's development. A writer has to develop a special sensitivity and a specified ideological position, in order to be able to show people in which direction the imagination is going.

Adeola: I have with me your collection of poems, *Daughter of My People Sing* and your two plays, *The Trial of Dedan Kimathi* (co-author, Ngugi wa Thiong'o) and *The Long Illness of Ex-Chief Kiti*. An obvious theme they all have in common is the call for a meaningful liberation in Africa. Obviously you are disillusioned with our so-called Independence. Is this disillusionment localized or can you see a common trend in our history of failure on this continent?

Micere: It is not localized. It is a history that is common to all formerly colonized people, most of whom, today, are neo-colonialists, promoting the very same structures as under colonialism. If you do a class analysis, a lot of the black people who are in power present precisely the same ideology of capitalism as the colonizer. This is my quarrel with the present day African intelligentsia. It is true that I am a member of the petit-bourgeoisie, a very privileged and elite person, because of my job as a university professor. But how can I be happy with my class position when the majority of my people are living in poverty. What arrogance have I to talk of myself as having succeeded?

Adeola: As a writer among other writers and other privileged people in Africa, do you find a nucleus of serious people who are working for change?

Micere: Most of our intelligentsia are liberals. We are ready to discuss things and to talk intellectually about issues. But when it really comes to a hard choice in which there is a clear struggle with the people against imperialist and capitalist forces, then we find reasons for escaping. A clear third are outright conservatives. Probably they make two-thirds, who knows? These reaped the fruits of Independence, so they are comfortable, and they feel they deserve to be privileged. Some of them may even rationalize that the workers are poor because they didn't have the brains to go far in their education, they are lazy, and so on.

The writer too has a class position. We have only a very few writers who have chosen to side with the oppressed majority, who have actually taken a clear ideological position in which they are going to use their writing as a weapon in the struggle for liberation. We have another category of humanistic writers, who feel very angry about the sufferings of the majority of our people, but who couch it in a very evasive way, in imagery, in their writing. Then, of course, there are those who tell you, 'I write for myself. I write for pleasure. My writing is my own business. It has nothing to do with politics'. The kind of writer that I have a lot of time and respect for is a writer like the late Alex La Guma. I admire the fact that his writing was not only talking about struggle, but he was really part and parcel of the struggle in South Africa. I admire somebody like Ngugi wa Thiong'o, whose example and position in life has demonstrated his commitment to the struggle of the Kenyan people. I admire somebody like Sembene Ousmane. This kind of writer I want to identify with.

Adeola: The examples you have just cited are great African writers who have had no problem being published in spite of their ideological position. Is this the experience of the majority?

Micere: No, it isn't. I'm very glad you point it out. The thing about western capitalists is that where profit will get into their pockets, they will not let a chance go. So that even when the books of somebody like Ngugi wa Thiong'o were very, very dangerous and nobody dared to touch them, Heinemann went ahead and published them, with all the risks involved, because they knew the books would sell. This is not the case with some of the younger and unknown writers. Some of them have great problems in getting anywhere near a publishing house. The majority of our people, who compose in our tongues and who cannot write, are even worse off. Their materials will first have to find a collector and then go through the publishing house. This is very difficult. That is why I said earlier that a lot of our writers are still unsung. We have not seen them, we have not seen their talents.

Adeola: To continue with the question of publishing, I have interviewed several women writers, both well known and unknown, most of whom complain about the problems they encounter with publishers. Some have been downright discouraged and have stopped writing. Do you have any ideas or suggestions as to what could be done about this problem?

Micere: The only position I can take on this will be that of someone who is thoroughly committed to socialism as an economic system. Under socialism you could organise your publishing houses as cooperatives, owned by the State, which would ensure that discrimination and repression did not take place. But so long as our publishing houses are owned by western capitalists or their local supporters, our problems will continue. They will go for writers who have big names, who will make money for them.

Adeola: I have spoken to some writers here in Zimbabwe and been told that, at present, anybody who writes will have no problem getting published. On the other hand, in places like Kenya and Nigeria, writers are saying that in the 1960's publishers were soliciting for manuscripts, but now it is a different story. Do you think the establishment of writers' cooperatives will guard against these discrepancies? Do you think the time will come when writers in Zimbabwe will experience the same problems as other African writers?

Micere: One exciting thing about being in Zimbabwe at this particular time is that, because the Government has declared socialism as its policy and has taken a clearly legislated party line, even publishing houses are very, very careful not to thwart any line that the Government has officially committed itself to.

Adeola: Do you think the struggle in South Africa is part of the same struggle as yours in Zimbabwe or is it at a different level?

Micere: The South African struggle is very close to us here in Zimbabwe, and is both impressive and uplifting. A people have said, 'We are moving forward and this is the way the stream is going to flow'. They have taken action against racism, against apartheid, and a lot of them understand that the true enemy, the chief contradiction that they are fighting, is the economic system under capitalism that impoverishes the majority. At a conference I attended in Oslo recently, Ellen Kuzwayo spoke with strength and determination about the struggle. The role of the progressive writer, who has aligned herself with the suffering majority, is to create a consciousness by the kind of poems, novels and drama she writes; to ensure that our people – workers and peasants, old women and men, and children – see themselves in the pages of those books. In bourgeois writing we don't see them, unless as servants, or supportive characters. So we want to give them a central position in our stories, novels, poems and plays, and to give them powerful and authentic voices.

So I see this as the role of the writer. But this role is not feasible if we see ourselves as speaking *to* the people. We can only speak *with* them and write *with* them. We are not gurus, translating what they say or what they do.

Adeola: *In Daughter of My People Sing*, a beautiful and inspiring collection of poetry, you challenge the youths to struggle to 'make a new earth'. Do you see part of the struggle for a new Africa the struggle to free her womenfolk?

Micere: Yes, surely. By her class position, the African woman occupies the lowest rung of the ladder. But on top of that, most of the women in Africa have grown up under patriarchy, in which the male principle is promoted and the female principle is repressed. So we are talking about a continent where women face at least two levels of oppression.

Adeola: Would you say that on the whole African women writers have confronted seriously the ultimate questions that literature attempts to explore: 'Who are we?', 'Why was I born?', 'What does life mean for me?'

Micere: I think that our women writers have wrestled with the questions in various ways. But women writers have not gone very far, really, beyond our male counterparts, in analysing the condition of the majority of oppressed women among the workers and peasants. Very often the women who are portrayed are from intellectual circles and the privileged class. So we are still speaking for the minority instead of the majority. My call to African women writers is to find ways and means of reaching the majority of our people, who are women, to speak for them.

Adeola: Will it damage the ultimate struggle for a complete social, economic and political liberation of Africa if we focus on singing the song about the oppression of women?

Micere: There is nothing wrong with singing about women but I think that we must be very careful to define and specify which women we are singing about. I still insist that we must sing and sing and sing again about our mothers out there in the rural areas, in the high density 'suburbs', and their poverty. This song can never be too much because it is the song of Africa. My only quarrel with singing is when we only sing for the well-known women, those who have made it in society, as if they represent the condition of all African women.

Adeola: *The Trial of Dedan Kimathi* focuses on the strength of women and their contribution to the liberation struggle in Kenya. Significantly, it is the Woman and the Girl (I am referring to the characters) who instil strength and courage into the Boy. In the same way, Kimathi attributes his strength to his grandmother in these words:

> . . . I was blessed by a blind grandmother.
> A peasant, a toiler.
> She imparted her strength, the strength
> of our people into me.
> I felt her blind faith, blind strength
> enter my bones. Fire and light.[1]

What is the purpose of this shift of focus from the great heroic figure of Kimathi to the women?

Micere: We didn't mean it to be a shift but a kind of fusion, to show that what Kimathi was fighting for was the same thing that a lot of our women were fighting for. Our concern was that whereas, the part that the men played in the struggle has been recorded by historians and biographers, the women on the whole have simply been forgotten. It is as if they were just sitting at the back somewhere and doing nothing. When I was doing the research on *Visions of Africa*, a thesis that was going to deal, among other things, with novels contrasting the colonialist–imperialist view with the vision of the insiders, and those committed to the people, this research revealed a lot of women who had actually served in the Mau Mau war as generals or lieutenants. Ngugi too had come across similar findings in his research. We even met some women who had worked very closely with Kimathi, and they were responsible for revealing to us the real character of the Kimathi that we depicted in the book, rather than the one presented by the colonialist: a Kimathi full of warmth, a great leader, a person who was really loved and respected. We did not meet anyone, man or woman, who did not love him, though they may have disagreed with some of the ways he carried out this or the other. The women were some of the strongest of the voices that told us what went on during the Mau Mau war. These voices gave us a vision, so we said the least we could do was to bring them out in the book and bring out this hidden strength. So we did it deliberately.

Adeola: Do you believe that each generation builds on a higher level? How do you view our generation in comparison with our mothers'?

Micere: I will tell you the honest truth. It depends on who we think we are, in terms of our class position. I think that the educated who are conservative and the educated who still have not aligned themselves with the impoverished majority of our people, have betrayed the position that our mothers and our fathers found themselves in thirty years ago.

I will tell you a story. There was a woman who witnessed a kind of quarrel, an illiterate woman who saw the educated women quarrelling for high position in the women's organizations. She stood up and made a very moving statement that I took note of. She said, 'Look, I do not have all those high degrees that you people have, but so long as you have them, they are mine. I feel they are as much mine as they are yours'.

You know, the workers and peasants, óur mothers and grandmothers, even as we are talking now, have so much faith in us. They believe we went to school in order to learn the secrets of the enemy. Progressive people are fashioning history, pushing history forward, because they can see the sacrifices that were made so that we are where we are today. I think this should be the task of any progressive writer.

Adeola: You have done this in *The Trial of Dedan Kimathi*. There are clearly stated challenges in the play. The Woman challenges all women to be involved in the struggle when she says:

> The trial of our strength.
> Our faith, our hopes, our resolve
> The trial of loyalty
> Our cause. (p. 14)

Kimathi's challenge is to all when he tells the Business Executive:

> We shall win the war. For, let me tell the fainthearted that this our struggle will continue until we seize back the right and the ability to make ourselves new men and women in our own land. (p. 45)

It is a unique play, one that takes us close to the theatre of Brecht and plays like *Mother Courage*. It is a theatre of consciousness-raising and encouragement to struggle. What sort of reactions have you got from people concerning the play?

Micere: When we wrote the play we were very conscious of our positions as lecturers and writers. We were using drama specifically in order to conscientize our people, to review our history with them and theirs with us to be able to answer the questions, 'Where are we?' and 'Where are we heading?'

Adeola: Most critics believe that Ngugi's creative talents are to be appreciated more in his fiction than his drama; could one then attribute the success of *The Trial of Dedan Kimathi* largely to you?

Micere: You are being a typical female critic. Quite a lot of male critics assume that because Ngugi is a famous writer, he is the sole writer and spirit behind *The Trial of Dedan Kimathi*. I don't think that it has occurred to any of them that I have been writing since school under Rebeka Njau, my involvement in drama goes back to the age of eight years. Those who realise this sing a different tune. Since the book has been published, Ngugi and I have tried to show that it is a collective effort. It is immaterial to say who came up with the idea – we were living through the same problem, the same issues in the struggle. Ngugi mentions this in his latest book, *Decolonizing The Mind*.[2] He and I would agree with what those people who broke through the door of the theatre said, that it was *their* story. We just added poetic licence and dramatic form to it.

Notes

1. Ngugi wa Thiong'o and Micere Githae Mugo: *The Trial of Dedan Kimathi* (UK: Heinemann, 1977), p. 36.
2. Ngugi wa Thiong'o: *Decolonizing the Mind* (UK: James Currey, 1986).

Rebeka Njau

Rebeka Njau was born in Kenya. She was educated at Alliance Girls' High School and Makerere University. She has been a teacher, textile designer, an artist and a writer. She works in Nairobi with the Kenyan Council of Churches as a researcher and editor. This work allows her time for the type of research she is interested in and she has drawn materials for her writing from this research. Her publications include *The Scar* (1965) *Ripples In the Pool* (1975) and *Kenyan Women and Their Mystical Powers* (1985). She is at pains to explore the essence of traditional life, which gave dignity and meaning to the life of our fore–parents and which we are in danger of losing.

10
Rebeka Njau

This interview was recorded at Church House, in Nairobi where Rebeka works as a researcher and editor, on 30 June 1986.

Adeola: You are a distinguished African woman, who incorporates in her one life the roles of teacher, mother, artist, writer and worker. Could you tell me how you have managed to handle all these aspects of your life?

Rebeka: When I was a student at school, I wanted to be a dramatist. I wanted to go on the stage. I discovered I couldn't do that, but perhaps if I became a teacher, I might find some opportunity to work with the students and do drama. So I trained as a teacher and taught for many years, before I decided that teaching was too taxing. I needed to do something easier, so that I could find time to write. The opportunity came when I gave up being headmistress of a girls' secondary school and turned into a kind of . . . I don't call myself an artist, but I've always been interested in colour and design, and that sort of thing, and I got involved in textile designing – tie and dye, batik, that kind of thing. At the same time, I found more time to write because there were no school books to mark. And then I am lucky, I have a small family, only two children, and I always found somebody to help me with them, therefore it wasn't too difficult for me. It is still very taxing to be creative. I've found myself that I have to write at night.

Adeola: You have published a novel, *Ripples in the Pool*, some plays, and more recently a book, *Kenyan Women and Their Mystical Powers*. What determines the choice of themes in your writing?

Rebeka: First of all, I wrote a play, *The Scar*, when I was in Uganda. I can tell you a bit about the background. I came home to Kenya from Uganda and at home I heard a very sad story from my village, about

103

a woman who had never got married but had a child. Her parents wanted her to get married, her brothers wanted her to get married, but she never got married. The father got very sick and when he was just about to die, he called the sons, and also this young woman, and divided his land among all of them, including the girl who had never got married. Soon after that, he died. After his death the brothers were very angry. They felt that their father should not have left a piece of land for their sister, that she should have got married. They started fighting amongst themselves and the mother was very sad about the whole thing. You know the sister committed suicide! When I heard this story I really felt so bad. See what injustice there is! Why, just because she is a woman she should get married, she should not stay there. So when I went back to Uganda I just found myself creating a play.

Now about the recent book, *Kenyan Women and their Mystical Powers.* I have always been disturbed by people who say that the women who are highly educated have copied western ideas, knowing that my own strength comes from inside myself and from my own background, from my mother whom I respected very much, and grandfather, who I knew when I was a very small child. I wanted to go back into that history to find out if there were any strong women who were respected by men and who were not just seen as women. I wanted to prove that there must have been. I did not know where to begin. It was a kind of groping in the dark because you could never hear that there was any woman of any special merit in the past, although they were taking part in traditional religion and so on. So after travelling around, researching my topic, I enquired whether there was a road or a village named after a woman. Somebody told me, 'Oh, yes, there is such a village, that village is called by this name, that is a woman's name'. Why should it be called that? I started investigating and I discovered that she was a highly respected woman in the past. The old men I interviewed all spoke very highly of her, not as an ordinary woman, rather as a woman they respected because she had certain powers. So, that is how I continued. I started with my own tribe, my own group because it is easier when you can speak the language. After discovering several women, I went to the Kenyan National Archives here to see whether there was any mention of women anywhere, either in early reports or in letters from Provincial Commissioners and District Commissioners. These were colonial administrators. You know there were all those letters they wrote about the country. I read some of them to see whether there was any mention of a woman. If there was a mention, I then tried to go out and check who that woman was.

Adeola: You are one writer that has consistently focused on women in your writings. *The Scar, Ripples in the Pool* and *Kenyan Women*

Heroes, all have women at the centre. When you write, do you deliberately try to preserve certain kinds of images of the African women?

Rebeka: You know, I don't know. First of all, because I am a woman, maybe I understand a woman through my emotions much more. But also when I write, I don't just say I am going to depict a woman in this book, it would depend on what really has moved me to write. If I know there is some injustice being done somewhere and it concerns a woman, I just find a woman featuring. Now . . . in this other novel I'm halfway through, the main character is not a woman, but a woman plays a big role as an inspiration for the man there. I don't think she ends up in a tragic way. I think she will give a very good lesson and an inspiration to a man. But this time it is a man, an artist, who is playing the key role. I also have a woman who is very creative, a traditional woman who has not gone to school, who makes pots. She is a traditional potter and she is going to play a very big role here.

Adeola: Do you write from experience, from real life or do you try to rearrange what you observe in real life?

Rebeka: Not really, there is a lot of imagination in what I do. People who have read my book *Ripples in the Pool*, some of them, . . . I know for example somebody who could not finish it saying, 'That is not really you. I can't imagine you writing something like that'. So you don't go around with your eyes closed! Something that I have felt very strongly cannot leave me. Recall what I told you about *The Scar*, how the inspiration came about. So I can't say what I write is factual, but of course you cannot write without looking at what is going on in life.

Adeola: Your female characters are strong and progressive, yet they end tragically. I'm thinking of Mariana in *The Scar* and Selina in *Ripples*. Why is this?

Rebeka: Well, I don't know. Maybe that was a phase I was going through. I've been thinking about women's situation. Whatever they do, it is not appreciated, they are not fulfilled. That is why I have decided to look at women of the past and ask, how did they make it? What did the men see in them to value, fear and respect? I have learnt a great deal.

Adeola: So, you will agree with me that we are living in a disillusioning world where all the hopes we had in Africa at Independence seem to have been dashed? How do you relate to this environment of failure in your writing?

Rebeka: I can say I have been disillusioned about many things. It may be because of the way I was brought up myself. I remember my mother was very strong. I come from a big family. There are twelve of us, five sisters and seven brothers. There was no difference in the way my mother treated all of us. Going to fetch water, we all went including my brothers; cooking, we all did it. If there was a farm to cultivate, my mother would measure it out, a piece for me and a piece for you, whether you are a boy or a girl. That was the way we lived, there was no difference and there was respect. When I got married I never thought I would be made to feel that 'You are a woman, you are inferior'. That came to me as a kind of shock. I started feeling disillusioned about life. I started wondering, 'If you have a brain, if you want to think and be yourself, have your own ideas; how do you go about things?' You find it very difficult to fit into marriage with these kind of views. This is my disillusionment. It may not be true with other people, but from what I have observed, here in Kenya and also what I have observed about other people in Africa, we still have a very long way to go to develop certain values; in order to feel that we have our own values and are not copying anybody, are not apologising. I am looking forward to the time that we will say, 'O.K., you are a woman, you are not the copy of anybody'.

Adeola: Do you have any particular audience in mind when you write?

Rebeka: I write for the general public. I don't consider writing for schools alone because that's where the market is. I consider my writing suitable for everybody, but I have the African audience in mind, I am not writing for outsiders.

Adeola: Your writing seems to be more for adult readers, or have you found young people reading and enjoying it?

Rebeka: You know on Saturday I went to a rally with a certain lady and her daughter. The daughter wants to read *Ripples in the Pool*. I will give it to her to read because she told me she has borrowed it from somebody else and they were all reading it, but she didn't finish it. I want to try it on her. In our office here, there is a young girl who read *Ripples in the Pool* and she said she enjoyed it very much. So we can say that from above the age of 13, Form I onwards, they should be able to read it.

Adeola: In a review of *Poems of Black Africa* (U.K.: Secker & Warburg, 1975) that you wrote several years ago, you made some very strong statements. You insisted that:

> African literature must communicate. Art for art's sake is a luxury a country like ours can hardly afford. Writing that is mere intellectualism is not for a country that is full of social ills and miserable poverty. And when we consider that most of African writing ends up in schools where it is consumed for examination, African writers must make sure they know their audience before they take up a pen to write.[1]

That article was published ten years ago. Are you satisfied with the development of African literature in the light of your concern about the commitment of the writer to her African audience?

Rebeka: I'm not yet satisfied. We should be writing more and more and I still believe that when you write you must communicate, you must write simply, for people to be able to understand. You shouldn't use obscure language, especially if you are writing in a foreign language, as we are, writing in English. Who are you going to communicate with if your language is not clear? I wish I could be writing in my own Kikuyu language but then I know that, I have a bigger audience if I write in English. So I feel we really are not in a position to analyse our own writing, especially here in East Africa. We haven't written enough for people to be able to say, 'This is the trend of East African writing'.

Adeola: You say that in East Africa people have not written a lot. But even in the little that has been written, the male voice dominates. Why is this? Why is it that we have no women to compare with an Achebe, an Ngugi, a Soyinka?

Rebeka: I think the problem with us is that we are not brave enough. We churn out simple things, wondering, 'If I express myself like this, what will people think?' We fear to turn ourselves inside out. If we become courageous enough to come out and write on social or political issues, our voices will be heard. But I think women are afraid, also they are overburdened with a lot of work. Time is not there; they have too many children and they are busy looking after the family in the evening, and working during the day. And you look odd if you say you are going to wake up in the night to write, you don't look like a woman.

Adeola: It is not easy at all, it takes a lot of discipline.

Rebeka: Yes, it takes a lot of discipline. Let me give you an example. One man, a church man, when he saw *Ripples In The Pool* he said, 'You didn't write this book, it is your husband who has written it'. I was so shocked.

Adeola: You are the second writer to narrate this type of experience. Asenath Odaga too was told that her husband was writing her books for her.

Rebeka: A journalist friend who read my book told another journalist friend, 'That woman, she is a woman and a half'. When I asked what it meant to be a woman and a half, I was told, 'just to be able to write like that, you are more or less like a man'. Perhaps he felt that only men should think deeply, while women are supposed to write on simple subjects.

Adeola: Do you think the men writers speak for us?

Rebeka: No, they look at the traits they want in a woman and that is the kind of woman they portray. A woman who is most concerned about beauty and dresses, a woman who wallows in a brothel. But a woman who has personality and strength of the spirit never features, because they are afraid of that kind of woman.

Adeola: Can you tell me what it is, in your background, that has enabled you to become a writer?

Rebeka: Well, let me tell you, it was fight from my childhood, the way I was brought up. I was brought up in a Christian home. Also my grandfather used to live far away from us. During the school holidays my mother sent us to him. He turned out to be a man with a clear mind in his old age. The old man was a perfectionist. When he went to his farm to cultivate, he would crawl on the ground turning the soil, not a weed could remain. He was so thorough. There were so many things he used to tell us. Then, I used to meet girls in the village who had never been to school, who were living in the traditional way. They used to take me through the forest, and show me insects, tell me, 'If you do this, this will happen'. So I sort of lived two lives. That world inspired me and I would want to express it. But I was a very shy person, and I don't express myself very well, except in writing. I found my medium either to be writing or acting. So I can say my inspiration came from a long time ago. And I don't write because I want people to know me, I write because there is something I want to express. Whether my books are published or not, that I don't worry about. I must finish a piece of work.

Adeola: What barriers or constraints did you have to grapple with in order to achieve your goal as a writer?

Rebeka: As a writer you have to think freely, and you have to endure all these people looking at you and describing you as odd. If you are not strong you will give up. 'Why don't I conform?' you ask yourself. The society expects a woman to behave in a certain way. But as a writer you just cannot conform. You are overburdened. For instance, I have to work in this office, and I have very little time to write. But you cannot give up the struggle. It is what I am committed to.

Note

1. Rebeka Njau, review in *East Africa Journal*, 1976.

Flora Nwapa

Flora Nwapa was born in eastern Nigeria in 1931. She has the honour of being a pioneer, as the first African woman writer to publish a novel. She received her basic education in Nigeria, and in 1953 she attended Edinburgh University, where she received a diploma in education. Teaching, government and publishing are other occupations she has engaged in, in addition to writing, proving her own belief in the need for the African woman to be versatile for her own survival. Her best known novels are *Efuru* (1966) and *Idu* (1969). Other writings include *This is Lagos and Other Stories* (1971), *Never Again* (1976), *Wives at War and Other Stories* (1980) and *One is Enough* (1981).

11

Flora Nwapa

Flora Nwapa was interviewed at the conference on The Black Woman Writer and The Diaspora, East Lansing, Michigan, 28 October 1985.

Adeola: You are the first published African woman novelist and you are one of the very few women who write. I believe that many more people want to write but they have some kind of impediment in their way, something stopping them from taking the plunge.

Have you found writing to be a lonely act? Do you have to be lonely to be a successful writer? Is there a conflict between your communal life as an African who recognizes that the essence of your life is derived from the community and the life you have imposed upon yourself as a writer?

Flora: Writing is lonely in the sense that you sit down in your room, you lock yourself up and you stay and sweat it out for hours on end, depending on how your inspiration is at that particular time. In that sense it is a lonely act.

Adeola: But in terms of the African way of life how do you find the time 'to sit and sweat it out'? What about the demands of the family and the extended family?

Flora: This is the problem facing us in Nigeria. People ask, 'How come we do not have more Nigerian women writers?' My answer is that a Nigerian woman faces far too many problems in our society today. She goes to the university to get qualified, when she finishes she gets a job. Then she gets married. Within a short while she starts having children. Then she has to look after her children and her husband and she also has a job to do. As you rightly said, the extended family comes in. She might be expected to send her younger brothers and sisters to school. How does she do all these? The problems are compounded when, in the situation that we find ourselves today, she has to go out and look for essential commodities, things like milk, soap to wash her clothes and bathe herself, all the things you need in the house. If she doesn't go to get these things, she will face starvation. So she finds it very very difficult.

Adeola: But how have you overcome these problems?

Flora: Things were much easier during our time. I graduated in 1957, then I went to Edinburgh and came back in 1958. By the end of 1958, I was already working. It wasn't difficult at all to get a job then. Educated people were privileged; by the time you returned from overseas, the job was waiting for you. You were not even expected to apply. They would look for you and ask you to attend an interview, which was a formality. You got the job in a very short time. That same week, I got a car, I got a driver. I didn't have up to £3 in my pocket when I got all these. When I went to my work place in Calabar, there was a big house waiting for me and everything was there. I took my sisters with me.

Adeola: That was during the colonial period, and you were one of the lucky ones.

Flora: Yes, we were the lucky ones. Today everything has changed. After Calabar I taught at Queen's College, Enugu. Then it was single-stream classes where you had to teach some thirty children. I was methodical and properly organised; by the beginning of Easter I had prepared my lessons and my exams for the following term so that I had a lot of time on my hands.

Adeola: When did you start writing?

Flora: I started when I was teaching. I must have had about thirty–five periods a week, but I felt that it wasn't enough. When I got home I discovered that there was nothing for me to do. Then I began to scribble, to write things about my school days. I stumbled into writing *Efuru*. That was how I started.

Adeola: As an African woman writer, are you concerned about the fate of the black woman and the future generation?

Flora: I am quite concerned about the fate of the black woman, whether she is in Africa, North America or the Caribbean. She faces many problems. I think the crux of these problems is economic. If the black woman is economically independent she and her children will suffer less.

Adeola: In spite of nearly three decades of Independence, and tragic experiences like the civil war, we Africans are still a people with no direction and we are not taken account of. In fact, we are often despised. To what extent do these realities affect your work?

Flora: How does this reality affect my work? I suppose you mean the reality of being an under-dog. Spiritually, it does not affect my work, but physically the question of getting the tools that I need to do my work affects me.

Adeola: Do you feel that through your writing you can address the problem of underdevelopment?

Flora: Yes, I can do that. But I don't want to arrogate a solution to myself. It is arrogant to say that I want to do this or that to save the world.

Adeola: But as a Nigerian, how do you feel about the progress we have made?

Flora: The problems we face in Nigeria are not unique to us, they are problems of nation-building. Rome was not built in a day. If we look into the history of many nations we find that they have come through the stages we are passing through.

Adeola: So you are still hopeful?

Flora: I am very optimistic that things will not continue the way they are. When people say, 'But we have been Independent for twenty-five years', I ask, 'What is twenty-five years?' Look at Britain, they had the Wars of the Roses. If you think of all the European wars, and of the War of American Independence, you can see that our problems are not unique. It took the others so many years to reach their present stage of development. But the problem is that we became Independent when the others were already far advanced, so how do we catch up with them?

Adeola: We are being told we are underdeveloped, we are confused, corrupt and so on.

Flora: It is left to us. I always say that the fact that we have built sky-scrapers is not a sign of development. Development is not reflected merely in the physical structures, it is mental. The physical things you can build in two years but the mind – you cannot take just two years to develop it.

Adeola: What about our own civilization from where you take material for your writing, that was developed, was it not?

Flora: In certain areas it was developed. The Yoruba culture was developed. You had your system of Obaship, as they had in Benin. In the North they had the Emirs. In Igboland, for example, there was nothing like the kingship system, apart from in remote places like Onitsha, Aro and Opita where they gave allegiance to somebody they called the king. In other, smaller, areas of Igboland you owe allegiance to your own group. The head of the family is the one you look up to. These are the problems that face us. Then we were overcome by this 'Oyinbo' (white man). It is the problem of the 'Oyinbo' (western civilization) that has overwhelmed us.

Adeola: In one word, you have hope for the future generation. Let me put the question differently. Your children, in what type of Nigeria do you think they will live? Will they be faced with the kind of struggle you have tried to expose in your writing, against the oppression of women?

Flora: The oppression of women starts in the home. In our homes today, we treat girls differently, and we treat boys as if they are kings. I remember the problem I have in my own home when I make my only son go to the kitchen and cook, wash the plates and so on. He does it. But then my mother-in-law comes in and says in a raised voice, 'Why are you allowing this boy to do this, he is a man, he is not supposed to be in the kitchen'. That is where the trouble stems from, the double standard we use in bringing up our children. There was another encounter that I was very happy about because my son was then only about five years old. Grandmother told him that he was not supposed to be in the kitchen. Then he replied, 'Grandmother, but Amos is our cook and Amos is a man'. If you can educate a boy at an early age he will grow up to appreciate women, and to appreciate his wife. You see this is very very important. A woman who says she is oppressed and then has a son and treats him like a king, such a woman is perpetuating the problems we are complaining about.

Adeola: What in your own life is responsible for your becoming a writer?

Flora: Some writers say that they wrote because they had an initial wound. Others say they've always wanted to be a writer, that it was their ambition, like my friend Buchi Emecheta. I didn't have that kind of ambition. Writing is something that I started doing by accident rather than by design.

Adeola: Have you found fulfilment in writing?

Flora: If I had not found fulfilment in writing I would not have continued to write. It is something that has given me a lot of satisfaction.

Adeola: 'To be black and to be a woman is a double ill-fate'. What is your response to that?

Flora: In Britain, America and Europe it is not so. But in Nigeria that statement is relevant. You are oppressed at home, you are oppressed at work. Your husband oppresses you, your employer oppresses you and then your society piles upon you double, if not treble suffering.

Adeola: How do male writers regard you?

Flora: The writers? If you talk about the Nigerian male writers, we have a very good relationship. They don't feel threatened at all. But the critics? I won't say that they have been too kind. A friend of mine, Ama Ata Aidoo, brought this out very clearly in a paper she presented at one time. She said that some male critics don't even acknowledge female writers. Every artist thrives on controversy, so you are killing the writer if you don't even talk about her. Being ignored is worse than when you are even writing trash about her.

Adeola: Is there any particular message in your work?

Flora: I think the message is, and it has always been, that whatever happens in a woman's life . . . marriage is not the end of this world; childlessness is not the end of everything. You must survive one way or the other, and there are a hundred and one other things to make you happy apart from marriage and children.

Adeola: How has this message been taken by your readers?

Flora: Well I wouldn't know. It is for you critics to examine that.

Adeola: It is an important message and you will realize that it differs from the attitude of our parents' generation. You know that to be childless in the past was regarded as a tragedy. So, if even nothing else was achieved by your writing, that message, contained in your novels, is a very important one.

Now, what barriers both inward and outward, do you face in attempting to produce literature?

Flora: I don't have any barriers at all.

Adeola: Do you have enough time to devote to your writing?

Fiora: Now I have less time because of the publishing business that I have set up. But I hope that I will be able to find someone who can look after the publishing side whilst I get on with my writing.

Adeola: There was a break of some years between your earlier novels and the more recent ones. Have you seen any significant development between your first two major novels, *Efuru* and *Idu* and the later ones?

Flora: *Efuru* was published in 1967. Then we had the civil war. But before then I had already written *Idu*, which was published in 1970. Because of that I knew that I would have continued and I might have written two or three novels had the war not intervened. There are people who write when there is a crisis, but I found that I could not write when there was a war going on. It was not because there was no paper. There was this problem of instability. You didn't know where you were going the next day. You didn't know whether the Federal troops were going to come and drive you from your home to a refugee camp. So, that sort of uncertainty did not encourage the creative process. Then, at the end of the war, I was made a minister in the East Central State government. The job was overwhelming, but even at that time I was able to produce the short stories, 'This is Lagos' and 'Never Again'.

Adeola: Do you notice any substantial change in your writing, say for example, in the way you perceive the world?

Flora: I haven't. The only difference is that whilst *Efuru* and *Idu* are set in my home town of the late 1940's and early 1950's, my next novel, *One is Enough* is set in a more contemporary time. Amaka, the heroine, who operates both in Onitsha and Lagos, is not the same type of heroine as Efuru and Idu. My heroines have changed because of the change in circumstances.

Adeola: In the earlier novels, you addressed the problems that women faced in traditional society. But in *One is Enough* the exigencies of the fast society, their effects on the African woman, are examined.

Flora: Yes, that is what I tried to do.

Adeola: Do you read much of other writers?

Flora: Yes, I do, quite a lot. I read Buchi Emecheta and I read African–American and Caribbean writers, such as Toni Morrison, Alice Walker, Paule Marshall – there are great similarities.

Adeola: You are obviously a very strong woman, undaunted by circumstances, whom many people admire. Where do you derive all this strength from?

Flora: (laughs) Maybe from God who gave me the physical strength and the opportunities that I have had. And then from my parents, who brought me up in the best traditions. From my stars, for making me a Capricorn. Those of us who are Capricorns are not only energetic, but when we set our minds to something we hold on to the very end. We don't give up easily.

Adeola: Your novels are very much based on Igbo mythology and folklore. How did you come to know these folk beliefs?

Flora: Having been brought up by parents who had strong Christian beliefs and who rejected anything that was not Christian, I had a unique opportunity of living with my grandmother in a polygamous environment. She was one of seven wives and within a very short time I learnt a lot about things I would not have learnt if I were staying with my parents. My grandmother too was a Christian, but had been converted after having all her children, so that all the traditional practices and beliefs were still with her. In such a large family there were so many children to play with, moonlight nights and all the rest of it. My mother would never have allowed us to play during the moonlight nights, because it is believed that young girls misbehave. I was 17 then and I learnt a lot about our traditions.

It was from there too that I got the idea of Efuru running away to get married when the bride price was not paid. In my home town in the 1930's and 1940's, it was very common for a young girl to elope. I think I owe all this to the fact that I lived with my grandmother.

Adeola: How do you see yourself in the development of African literature? You know that you have inspired and encouraged other people just as Achebe has done.

Flora: Achebe has inspired all of us. I remember when I first met Buchi, in her books; she said when she first started to write her husband burnt her manuscript and said, what did she think she was doing, how dare she to think that she could write, she was just a second class citizen in England. She replied that Flora Nwapa was a Nigerian. 'She is a woman, she has written'. But he told her that Flora Nwapa was writing in Nigeria, not as a second class citizen.

Adeola: So that is how she got the title of one of her best novels? This is interesting.

Flora: And then whilst she was away, this man took her first manuscript and set it on fire: These are some of the ways we inspire one another. It is heartening to think that in spite of that great setback,

Buchi didn't give up because there was a Flora Nwapa.

Adeola: Which of your writings is closest to your heart?

Flora: I can't say. Chinua Achebe put it this way, that it is like asking a father which of his children he likes best. One shouldn't ask that.

Adeola: Virginia Woolf wrote, 'I do my best work and feel most braced with my back to the wall', that it is in adversity and under compulsion that one does one's best work. Do you sympathize with this?

Flora: Yes, I do sympathize with that.

Adeola: In that case all of us should be writing because being women we have our backs to the wall all the time.

Flora: Yes, that is true but some people cannot sit in one place for one hour. You cannot write if you cannot face your own aloneness and sit down in a room by yourself for one hour. If you don't have that discipline, how are you going to be a writer?

Adeola: At the time when you were writing your novels tell me how your day was spent. Maryse Conde, the Guadaloupian writer, says she locks herself up. When her husband goes to work and the children go to school she clocks in at 9 a.m. and clocks out at 6 p.m.

Flora: It is not all that strict with me. When I have something to say and it comes I can sit down at my desk and do six hours at a stretch. Then for the next two or three days I will not want to go near that paper. I do not write at night at all, I prefer to get up at 5 o'clock in the morning, write for two or three hours and then go to work at 8 o'clock. But then I must go to bed between 8.30 and 9.30.

Adeola: What would be your advice to young African women who want to write? You agree that we do not have enough writers?

Flora: If you had asked me this question six months ago, I would have told you that we had enough writers. But my experience has shown me that we do not have enough writers. Late last year and early this year I have been bombarded by manuscripts sent for publication. When I sat down to confront them, most of them were very disappointing. I was so disillusioned when I discovered that about 75 per cent of the manuscripts I received were trash.

Adeola: So people are writing but they are not writing anything worthwhile?

Flora: No. They are not writing English as you and I know it.

Adeola: What then would be your advice to these writers? Apart from the language, what about the content?

Flora: There was a boy who told me he was writing a book. From the way he spoke I realised his spoken language was poor but I thought perhaps his writing might be better, so I asked him to send his manuscript. It was about armed robbery and drug-trafficking in Nigeria, which could have made interesting reading. But it was very poorly written. Besides, it is mainly men who are submitting manuscripts, not women. This is a pity.

Joyce Ochieng

Joyce Ochieng is an aspirant writer. She is Kenyan and she works at the University of Nairobi Library. She is in her twenties, sensitive and determined to make a success of writing because she has important things to preserve, though presently the possibility seems far off. She has instructive comments about established writers and her courage could be inspirational.

12

Joyce Ochieng

This interview was conducted with Miss Ochieng in the Cafeteria of the University of Nairobi where we met by accident on the 24th June, 1986.

Adeola: What you are reading seems like a manuscript of a book, are you a writer? Do you write poetry or novels?

Joyce: I don't write poetry. I could never understand poetry. I write fiction, real experiences.

Adeola: Have you managed to publish any of your writings?

Joyce: No, that seems impossible these days.

Adeola: Have you tried to get help from established writers?

Joyce: No they have no time. They are so busy with their own lives.

Adeola: What do you do for a living?

Joyce: I work in the University Library.

Adeola: Would you like to be a full-time writer?

Joyce: I would love to write full-time but I know there will never be a time when I will be able to afford to do that.

Adeola: Who is your audience? Is it young people, people of your age group?

Joyce: I generally write for young people but I think that older people can enjoy what I write. For example, I thought my writing on John Mboya has a lot of message for the older generation.

Adeola: Can you tell me why you write?

Joyce: Writing keeps me occupied. I am not idle, I enjoy the research associated with the topic I write about and I learn quite a lot in the process of my research. Since I started writing I have also learnt to type. I think I have a message which compels me to write. At present I consider writing as a hobby.

Adeola: How did you start writing?

Joyce: Out of school, looking for a job for nearly a year – it was a very frustrating period, then I decided, maybe I can write. I started with translation. I had started on a book, then I dropped it.

Adeola: Have you finished that book?

Joyce: Yes

Adeola: What is it about?

Joyce: I haven't titled the book yet but I was talking generally about women saying what I feel, that education hasn't changed women much. It started this way – I went to the university toilet and it was so dirty that I could not believe it was educated women that had made the place so bad. Then I did some research on psychology, behaviour, attitudes and cultural background of some women. That is what I wrote about.

Adeola: Are you a university graduate?

Joyce: No, I am not.

Adeola: Who directed your research then?

Joyce: Nobody. I just found it a natural process to research into a subject before you talk about it. So I started researching on my own.

Adeola: Why did you not go to university?

Joyce: After I left school, there were many others in my family who needed help so I had to seek paid employment very early. Anyhow, one doesn't really have to be at the university to improve one's education.

Adeola: That is quite true. But how did you find out how to go about your research?

Joyce: What gave me that background was bacause I had been a research assistant before. I had done research for a lecturer here on the women's movement and women's organisations, that gave me the ability to fish for materials.

Adeola: That explains it. But still you are very enterprising. Your main problem now is how to get your writings published. The manuscript in front of you right now, have you shown it to publishers? What is it about?

Joyce: It is on Human Development and Personal Dignity. When I finish correcting it I will send it to publishers.

Adeola: Can you tell me about its genesis?

Joyce: I was looking at life from a Christian perspective. I have read psychologists who discuss what motivates people to behave the way they do. Then I look at the Christian perspective and I compare both. I do a lot of writing on Christian topics.

Adeola: Do you have a problem publishing that type of writing?

Joyce: I don't care to publish them. I just write and keep them at home. I want my first published work to be that translation of John Mboya's writings. I consider it very significant historical and literary material.

Adeola: If the work is so important what is keeping it from being published?

Joyce: Actually it is with a publisher right now. The problem is that they are taking so long to make up their mind.

Adeola: Do you think it will help to have publishers for women writers only?

Joyce: I can see a need for setting up workshops to discuss these problems – problems facing a woman writer, the problem of publishing and so on. I have been reading something about that. Many people talk very well but they do not practise what they talk about. They say how they want to encourage young writers, but the minute you leave that workshop, nobody wants to see you. They take your manuscript and sit on it. I'd rather have my manuscript at home and be revising it.

Adeola: Is there any established writer that you enjoy reading?

Joyce: I read very widely and I have read all the books by Grace Ogot and Asenath Odaga. I can't say any particular one I like best – they express different views and address different audiences. I respect every writing as long as it is not a shoddy work.

Adeola: You know that there are more men writers in Africa than women. Have you ever wondered why this is so?

Joyce: I know the reason. Isn't the main reason that the men are the ones in publishing? If you go to someone's office today and he wants to date you before he looks at your manuscript, you feel frustrated. This won't be the case with male writers.

Adeola: Have you met other young people in the same position as yourself?

Joyce: Yes, they are just as frustrated as I am.

Adeola: In spite of all the disappointments and frustrations I hope you succeed. I look forward to reading your book one of these days.

Joyce: I hope that day will arrive.

Asenath Odaga

Asenath Bole Odaga was born in western Kenya. She studied history, education and literature at the University of Nairobi, where she also did her post-graduate work. She has attended several short courses abroad on writing and publishing, but her inspiration comes from her perception of her people's needs. Hence, she gave up a research position at the Institute of African Studies, Nairobi University, to devote her time fully to writing and publishing. Writing both in Luo and English, Asenath Odaga has published several books, including plays and fiction for children and adults. Some of her titles are *The Villager's Son, Jande's Ambition, The Shade Changes, A Bridge in Time, Between the Years, The Diamond Ring* and *Tutinda*. She has also published two works on oral traditions, *Yesterday's Today: The Study of Oral Literature* (1984) and jointly with K. Akivaga, *Oral Literature: A School Certificate Course* (1982). Her writings are well known in East Africa, where she is respected and loved for her dynamism. We stand to benefit from a wider circulation of these writings.

13
Asenath Odaga

This interview was conducted at Asenath's home in Kisumu, Kenya, on 29 June 1986.

Adeola: You started as a teacher and a researcher and you have published several books. Now you devote your time fully to writing and publishing. Can you tell me what led you into writing in the first place?

Asenath: What led me into writing is that as a young woman, when I trained to teach, I noticed that all the books the children read were written for European children. When I was at school I read books like *Lorna Doone* and *The Thirty-nine Steps* and I always wanted something based on our background and our experiences. I thought that children should have something to read about their background and the other children they know, real African heroes with whom they can identify. In the oral literature we have our own heroes. Of course, when the Europeans came, they thought this was not good enough and they introduced their own heroes. This was part of colonisation. So, I thought that for us to be really free, children must read about their own background, their own experiences, and make their own literature, just as we are making our own government.

Adeola: How does being black and female constitute a particular perspective in your work?

Asenath: To be black and female means that you are at a disadvantage in this world and in our society today. The fact that you are a woman means people feel that probably you are not equipped for whatever you are doing. Also you have so many other responsibilities. The wife has to rear the children, which is a hindrance to any woman's progress. Secondly, as an African woman there are

123

traditional beliefs and practices which put you down and make it difficult for you to be as free as if you were not married and not an African. You are all the time made to feel that your place is in the family and all the other things you are doing only come second.

Adeola: As you know, women writers are very few in Africa. You are one of those who have maintained a grip on this profession. What is it in your background that has enabled you to succeed as a writer?

Asenath: I come from a large family, we are seven sisters and two brothers. Our father brought us up on equal terms and gave us equal opportunities. All of us passed through high school and some of us have gone to university. Why I think I have succeeded is because I come from that firm background where it doesn't matter whether you are a boy or a girl, it is your ability that counts. My father always encouraged us to put our best effort forward in anything we were doing. I am fortunate, too, that when I got married, my husband never tried to put me down, he always allowed me. I say 'allowed' because in our society if a husband is against your progress you cannot get anywhere to develop as a person; he supported me. Together with my upbringing, I think these two things have played a great part in whatever success I might have achieved.

Adeola: What was your father's profession?

Asenath: My father was a teacher. He is now retired. My mother also went to school but she left early before acquiring any profession. The fact that our parents were educated helped us.

Adeola: Would you say that there are certain barriers, both inward and outward that you have had to grapple with over the years since you have been trying to write?

Asenath: Yes, there are plenty of them. When I first started publishing people thought that, being a woman, I couldn't write and that it was my husband who wrote the books and put my name on them. I had to make people realize that I was the one who wrote the books.

Secondly, being an African writer, one got the impression that people in education felt that anything produced by an African was inferior. So my readers set in our background were ignored because the education authorities still preferred books written by Europeans. Of course, the quality of language is better, one cannot doubt this. But it has been a major frustration that our own people do look down at our writing because they think anything African is inferior. (The writer points at her books displayed on the table).

Adeola: You have written quite a lot! I didn't find some of these titles in the library.

Asenath: *Jande's Ambition* is my very first book.

Adeola:What are the other titles?

Asenath: *The Villager's Son*. This is the latest – *The Storm*. It is quite an interesting story. I am now writing novels – the first one is *The Shade Changes*. Then I have two others that are ready for publication, one is called *A Bridge In Time* and the other one is called *Between The Years*. Then, of course, I have also done research on oral literature and have produced some work on it. The first I did was for children, *The Diamond Ring*, and then *Tutinda*. The latter is about the wisdom of our people, it is pronounced at the end of a story: 'tutinda'. It has no literal meaning, but roughly it says, 'these are the wisdom of our people, leave them as they are, grow on them and don't stay in this dump. You may add your own, but leave them as they are to form the core'.

In Kenya we place emphasis on oral literature in school. We didn't have any books in 1982 when it was first introduced in our high school syllabus. So together with a colleague of mine, Kichamu Akivaga, we produced the first book in oral literature for School Certificate.

Adeola: Kenya is the one country that I know of, where oral literature is taught in the education system right from school to university.

Asenath: It was being taught in the university for years, then we thought that it was illogical to start from the top and neglect the bottom. Even though they tell stories in primary schools, the academic discipline needs to be formalised. That is what is being done by the introduction of oral literature in the schools.

After publishing *Oral Literature for Schools*, I still had a lot of materials on the research I did at the University of Nairobi for six years, so I came up with another book in 1984 called *Yesterday, Today: the Study of Oral Literature*. It is different from the first book, this one is more about Kenyan oral literature. I have got more than one hundred proverbs in it, some riddles, about forty-one stories from all over Kenya and also lots and lots of songs. It also carries suggestions on how to go about doing your own interviews and what to take with you and so on. This is for higher forms at school and it is proving quite popular.

Then when I was doing my first degree I did a study of literature for children and young people in Kenya. I have published that also, it came out last year, 1985. Some of the oral literature collected lends itself to dramatization, so I write some of them in Luo and English. We took the drama to Nairobi and these too have proved very popular.

I have not neglected people from my group who do not speak English because I also write in Luo. Three works have been published in Luo, and there are six others which are not yet published. Some of the books are for new literates, who have just learnt to read. It tells them simple things about how to look after the children. Then our own folktales, I translated them into Luo for those who cannot read English.

I also have stories about our modern times. I have one called *Ogilo*. 'Ogilo, you can never put your arms around the wife', is the story of a little boy. I was commissioned by Heinemann to write two books for young people, and that is one of them. The boys like it very much.

Adeola: Is that book mainly for boys then?

Asenath: No, it is for young people generally. I have another one which talks about black marketing, poaching and the problems in modern society.

Adeola: You have written about a broad variety of subjects that cater for all types of audiences. You now have about twenty publications. How long have you been writing?

Asenath: I have about twenty-six publications. The first one came out in 1967, nearly twenty years ago. But there were times when I did not write at all. I became very critical of myself and I just could not write anything.

Adeola: How did you get over that period?

Asenath: I came to realise that you cannot be a perfectionist in this world, otherwise you won't write at all. There is nothing like a perfect book, just as there is no perfect person. So, I had to internalize everything and I accepted my limitations and continued writing. From around 1971 to 1980 I did not publish anything, I just could not. I wrote and put it aside.

Adeola: Were you miserable because you were not writing?

Asenath: I was not really miserable. I read a lot. I think it was a time of growth. I had to change. I realised that whatever I write can never be the ideal, may be a copy , it may even be a poor copy of what I had in mind. I learnt that lesson and now I write quite a lot.

Adeola: Can you tell me something about your creative process? Do you have any special time in the day or a special place where you go and write?

Asenath: Initially when my children were very small, when I returned from work, I would cook and we would all eat. By around 7.30 p.m. we had had our supper and then they did their homework. By about 8.30 p.m. they were in bed. We all did our homework together at that big table (pointing at it). My husband too was teaching at the Management College, so we all sat round the table together doing our work as a family. When the children went to bed, I remained and worked till around 11 p.m. When writing properly, creating, I like quietness. Then I go to bed and wake up at night when everybody is asleep and it is very, very quite. My brain works best then and I can create. Usually, I don't have any plan, I just start on a story and it works itself out. It starts and it goes on and on until I have it. One of the books you have in front of you, *A Bridge In Time*, is over 200 pages long. I just sat down and wrote it.

Adeola: How long did it take you to write it?

Asenath: Not very long. When I left the University of Nairobi in 1982, I came here to Kisumu and for ten months I didn't do anything else. I woke up very early in the morning, sat in that corridor and just wrote. I think it must have taken me a month to write it. Then of course, I put it aside and later on worked on it. What I normally do is to write the whole thing, put it aside, look at it again and then add on to it. I do this about three times. When I think it is good enough I have it typed.

Adeola: Do you work on one book at a time?

Asenath: No, I work on everything. For instance, now those two are finished, I want to produce a Luo-English Dictionary. I am working on that and I am also working on a Book of Proverbs of the Luo. I am also writing a book on tourism in Kenya. I don't approve of tourism at all. I have been doing a little research on what tourism is doing to Kenyans so I want to write about it, I have also started a publishing house, so during the day, I devote my time to reading manuscripts, at night I work on my own.

Adeola: Is it possible to be financially independent on writing?

Asenath: It is, but it is not easy. Even now that I have over twenty publications, the little money that I get from them I don't think could keep me if I didn't have a husband to support me as well. In Africa it is only Achebe and probably Ngugi and Soyinka who can live on their writings. But they are very few. I don't think there is an African woman writer who can live solely on her writing.

Adeola: When you write, are you particularly conscious of preserving certain kinds of images of African people?

Asenath: Yes, especially images of women. Long before I was aware of the women's liberation movement, I always liked to make my central female characters exemplary and very, very strong. For example, in my very first book published in 1967, *Jande's Ambition*, there is a girl called Jumomoshi. She is very strong and she helped the family quite a lot. I like a hero/heroine who is not perfect (as I have said there is no perfection in this world) who makes mistakes but is also able to learn from them. Even today, in western literature you still see Africans being type-cast as villains who kill people indiscriminately.

Adeola: The Tarzan image you mean? When the African is not stupid he is a villain. That trend still persists.

Asenath: Yes, it does. When it comes to using the intelligence even a child can outwit him. That is the picture of the African we still find in western literature. I think this is wrong. There are no superior human beings, we are all human beings with bad and good traits. So I try to make the African come out as a human being, not perfect but a person with weaknesses and strengths as well.

Adeola: You have published several books for children as well as books on oral traditions; now I have learnt from you that you have tried the novel form too. What determines your preferences?

Asenath: Somebody asked why writers are so conceited and why they feel they have something to say. I have been writing for too long for children, and I felt maybe I had a message also for adults. I write to entertain, to inform and maybe to chide the people. I have given the public about eighteen children's books, maybe it is now time for me to talk to the adults as well. Things are not all perfect in the adult's life, I may not be able to put things right, but I can be a commentator.

Adeola: You are a mother of five children who are also very accomplished. In Africa the traditional thinking is that a woman's responsibility is primarily her home. How have you managed to integrate your professional life, your home and your other responsibilities?

Asenath: Responsibilities?

Adeola: I am referring to your social responsibilities. I am sure you are very active in the society because almost everybody I have met knows you and speaks very warmly about you.

Asenath: I like people; I like to talk to them. I like to find out how they live, what makes them pursue a certain way. In fact, I think that is why I write.

It is not easy for a woman. There are not many educated women in the society so you feel a certain responsibility towards the less privileged. I am involved in several women's groups. In Kisumu we have the University Women's Association; we arrange lectures for the women around here, on health, agriculture and family life. All these activities do not prevent me from looking after my family, I have just had to work hard. As I said earlier, my husband has been very cooperative, we have worked together as a team. We have all learnt – the children and both of us as well. So it is quite possible to combine all activities if you plan properly and you are determined. I always feel that as you have only one life to live, if I give all my time to the children when will I myself learn and do something for myself? Maybe that is a selfish way of looking at it. But then I don't think it hurts them in any way. We all sit round the table, they do their work and I do mine. When I have fed them, talked to them and laughed with them, I may read them a story. Surely if then I send them to bed I won't be hurting them in any way at all. It seems to have worked quite well.

Adeola: What is their reaction to your being a writer?

Asenath: I think they like it. They always read what I write. Often they ask me, 'Mama, what are you working on?' I show them and they tell me whether they like it or not. I always try the books on them first.

Adeola: Have they encouraged you?

Asenath: Yes, they have. They have encouraged me quite a lot. Sometimes, they will offer to take over some housework saying 'We know you want to go and write'. I have acknowledged them in almost everything I have written because without them I wouldn't have been able to do it. Especially when I was doing my research, they were all very busy and yet I used to go out and sometimes stay away for a week, two weeks at a time; yet they accepted it.

Adeola: Have you been satisfied with the reception of your books?

Asenath: No. You know when you start writing, especially in an ex-colony like ours, people usually think, you are not English, so how can you write? They also feel that anything produced by an African is inferior. But I think now after twenty years they are accepting my work. The children's books sell fast, I can hardly keep up the stock. I run a little bookshop at the publishing house and even when you go to our biggest shop in Nairobi, they sell quite a lot of my books. Twenty years is a long time. Some of the children who read them then are now parents and they are recommending them to their children. So they are accepting them, just as people are now accepting things African because the imported ones are very expensive.

Adeola: Do you see any differences in the ways African male and female writers handle theme, character and situation in their writings?

Asenath: The male has always been dominant in Africa; this is their world, the society is theirs. What I do not like is the way men writers handle female characters in their books, in a way that makes them stupid or lazy or sensual. Of course, women writers also handle other women that way, but because most writers are men they have not given the African woman a very good image. I hope when more African women write they will try to give the African woman the dignity she deserves, and put her in her right place. She works very hard for it.

Adeola: Your answer has anticipated my next question. Do you feel there is a legitimate need to focus on women in your writing?

Asenath: As I have suggested before, there is that need to focus on women. We find that women do quite a lot in the family and in society as a whole. So I don't see why they should be put down by writers. In fact, somebody said that the future of our continent depends on women. You see that in many countries, at least in Kenya: the women are feeding the nation. The load is so heavy, still they manage to carry that load and improve the family as well, even though under a lot of strain.

Adeola: You wrote mostly for children at the beginning, now you are writing for adults. Is there any major difference between writing for adults and writing for children?

Asenath: It is very difficult to write for children because you have to watch the vocabulary, especially if you are writing in English. Also the statements you make, because if you are writing for young children, it is very easy to pervert their minds or to confuse their thinking. So it is more difficult to write for children than for adults. The story also has to be interesting. What interests an adult may not interest children at all. So you have to think very hard and plan before you write.

Adeola: So, then, you have your audience clearly in mind – if it is for children, which age group and whether it is for boys and girls: for the adults it is very general. But are you aiming your writing at an African audience first and foremost?

Asenath: I think I am writing for my society, for my people, the Africans. But as you know, literature is universal. The writer talks about human experiences which are identical in many places. For example, if you write about a woman in love or a woman who has lost a child – sorrow, love, happiness, injustices – these are universal experiences. Any good literature transcends a particular society and locality.

Adeola: Can you describe how your creative interests have evolved?

Asenath: I don't even know how, I have been at it so long. It is just than when I see something, I feel I would like to tell more people about my experiences and share what I have thought. Of course, as you grow older, you think and see much more. So, somehow, you also develop your thinking. Of course, lots of things happen in the society, and these are what form the materials for my writing.

Adeola: What have been the most crucial periods of your life as a writer?

Asenath: I think the period between 1971 and 1980. I was reading a lot, good and bad writing, philosophy. That was when I became very critical of myself and almost felt I would never write again, until I rationalized, as I explained earlier. It was the most crucial period of my life. It was very busy, my children were growing. There are times when a lot of demand is made on you as a mother; the children were just passing through their childhood into their teens. It is also the time when many fathers have very challenging jobs, a lot of responsibility. So I think that was a most crucial period.

Adeola: Many African writers, particularly women, have complained about their discouragement from writing by inadequate publishing facilities. Is this why you have set up your own publishing house?

Asenath: No, if this was the case I wouldn't have set up my own publishing house at all. After twenty years I am now recognized, I can publish, I am commissioned to write. But it is difficult to make a break-through because the publishers we have here are foreigners, multinationals. They are here not to develop local writers but to make money. They only accept what they think will sell internationally. If it is something local they accept it only when they are convinced that it will get into the schools.

As an indigenous writer, I am trying to start this publishing house so that I can encourage young writers and also create more literature for my people. The first thing I want to do is to publish a lot of books in the various local languages. Our government has passed a law that for the first four years of schooling, the children will learn in their mother tongue, Kiswahili, and the other local languages, of which there are about forty-one altogether. I have made an arrangement with somebody who has agreed to publish in all the major local languages and the first thousand copies of each will be given free to whichever group it is, then the rest they can buy from us.

I want to do it so that I can help in the development of our indigenous, Kenyan and African literature. Also to encourage young people to write and to encourage reading, because people will read when there is something to read. I won't make lots of money, but I hope I will make a lot of literature. The majority of illiterates are women, and it is about time we did something about this.

Adeola: How is this new job of setting up a publishing house affecting you creativity?

Asenath: It is very hard. I spend a lot of time wading through manuscripts, most of which are rubbish, not good enough. But because people have sent them I have to go through them. So this is taking quite a lot of my time. But, of course, I also have some readers. It is affecting my writing because I now have to share the time that I used to devote to my writing.

Adeola: Is it difficult setting up a publishing house?

Asenath: It is quite difficult and it requires quite a lot of money. I have had to get a loan from the bank.

Adeola: Yet it is not like other commercial ventures where you can realise your input quickly; it is really a labour of love.

Asenath: Yes, it is a labour of love. I tell people that a book is like a small baby. When it is small, nobody knows it, you have to go about introducing it to your relatives. It takes about two or three years before a book really finds a market, especially those that are not really for schools. Textbooks automatically have a market. But some of the other books have to be nursed and introduced to the readers.

Adeola: You are a very courageous person. I don't see anything in your background that pointed in this direction.

Asenath: Not at all. Some of my friends ask me, 'Asenath, why are you so brave?' Then I tell them, it is because I am a child of this world. I set my mind to do it; one of us has to do it and I think I should try and do it, just as anybody else could have done it.

Adeola: I know of Flora Nwapa who is trying to set up her own publishing house in Nigeria. I think you are setting examples for more people to follow.

Asenath: Oh, I tried to see her last year when she attended the Women's Conference, but I wasn't successful.

Adeola: When I spoke to her recently, she said she was having serious problems because she couldn't order equipment due to the foreign exchange problem in Nigeria. It is really very tough, but she has been able to put out more publications.

Asenath: She has. I saw some of them which the writer Mabel Segun brought to a conference in Germany. I don't have a press yet but maybe next year I will have one. Then my work will be easier.

Adeola: Did you have to undergo special training for setting up a publishing house?

Asenath: Yes, I did. In 1974–75, I worked with a church organization where I was their curriculum developer. During that time we had several seminars on writing which I attended. Again, in 1979, I attended a seminar in Cyprus. We were there for three weeks. We had somebody there who has set up a publishing house in Turkey and he talked to us. I went to that seminar with my mind made up to leave the university and set up my own publishing firm. So he taught us how to budget and what to do. Again, at the Institute of Adult Studies I attended a few courses on writing and at the German Goethe Institute. Of course, you can always be self-taught in these things – get a book and read it, talk to the publishers. Experience is the best teacher, as they say.

Adeola: You have done a lot of research into Dho-Luo oral traditions; your M.A. thesis is on *The Educational Values of Sigendini Luo* and you have also published an oral traditions reader for schools. What is responsible for this great interest in oral traditions, and do you derive the materials for your creative writing mainly from them?

Asenath: Yes. Our oral literature, the stories and proverbs I heard before I learnt to read, have formed my background. Some of these things the colonialists could not destroy completely; I felt we should resurrect them because of western education, we sometimes feel that our parents had nothing to offer us; that our background was hidden, pagan, primitive and backward. Why don't we help the younger people to see that not everything African is backward and primitive?

But not all my writing derives from oral literature. My first novel, *The Shade Changes*, is about a modern girl who goes to the university. The father forces her to marry his business partner. The girl rebels and goes to join her boyfriend in America. On the day of the marriage to the other man, her boyfriend comes and snatches her away. So you can see that not all my materials are from the oral traditions. We also have to give the children what is happening now. In that novel, I was also trying to say that we don't always have to accept our tradition. Women especially have to say 'no' sometimes to those traditions which put us down. Marriage is such a complex thing and it is for life. So because father says you must marry this man, you don't have to do it. Why do something to which you don't feel fully committed because your father wants it? These are some of the themes I take from contemporary life.

Adeola: Do you base your stories on events you actually know about?

Asenath: I create a lot from imagination but my imagination is sometimes based on things which happen. Actually, there is a girl who ran away on the day of her marriage. I heard the story, and I wove the story-line in the novel from the little episode I had heard.

Adeola: Have you had any reaction to your first novel?

Asenath: No, I haven't. It came out in 1984, so people are still reading it. We have sold about 800 copies, in Kenya and Tanzania. Some have also gone to Uganda. Those who read it like it very much. It is not the best but I thought I would start with something light, and I published it myself. I made it very cheap by producing it with news-print. It is not like a school text, for which you have to use very good material. It is cheaper than the average novel, which sells in Kenya today for 50 shillings ($US2.00); this is only about 25 shillings ($US1.00).

Adeola: My next question is based on your research paper, 'Popular Literature in East Africa'[1]. In that paper you made some controversial statements. Examining the popular Kenyan author, David Mailu's novels, you said, 'Women are depicted far worse then men. They are either prostitutes . . . victims of the emergent money-crazy society which dehumanizes practically all its members. The women are shown as being sensual, over-sexed, and perverted, victims of the bosses . . . Even the "mamas" are not spared. They are depicted as dissatisfied wives, who are ever at war with their erring and unfaithful husbands'.

You objected very strongly to this picture presented to the youth for consumption, saying that, 'Popular literature of this type is dangerous and harmful since it plays down all the other virtues which man should cherish and which puts him on a higher plane than animals'. 'What is needed', you suggested, 'is literature with some serious thoughts geared towards developing positive national ideals aimed at bettering the lives of individuals in the society as a whole'.

From the above statement one grasps your view that literature should be functional – moulding ideals and showing values that are worthwhile. Are such motives concretized in your own literary activities?

Asenath: Yes, very much so. That analysis summarizes my writings as well as my views on life. My objection is that when Mailu, or writers of 'Popular Literature' generally, write, they seem to depict only the perverted, the seamy side of human life. They play down the many virtues which even that particular character they are depicting may have. Therefore, I was saying that we should not present just a one-sided argument. That is what I mean by having a rounded character, who embodies both bad and good traits, because that is how we are as human beings.

Adeola: I would like to know the attitude of people to that research paper when you presented it.

Asenath: It was very controversial. I was very much criticised. Even someone who was not present at the seminar, a publisher, wrote and said that we were better off with local trash than with imported trash. But I replied that trash is trash.

Adeola: I think your point about the negative aspects of popular literature need to be restated, because since then that type of literature has flooded the market throughout Africa. I am referring specifically to Macmillan's Pacesetter series, which I consider very dangerous.

Asenath: Yes, it is very dangerous and it is here in Kenya as well. We don't write many here, most of them come from West Africa.

Adeola: People have been pointing out the problem of recolonizing our minds, particularly the minds of our youths. But it seems that the financial profit for the producers of this rubbish is the dominant consideration.

Asenath: They import them here wholesale. This is not doing anything good for our people. They are being read, but are taking a long time to catch on. That is why, if we had money to produce something good ourselves, we might arrest this trend. But it all comes to the question of our own 'big' people who are now the directors. They are part of the racket, they allow the rubbish to be imported. It is very unfortunate.

Adeola: I raised it at a conference on African literature at the University of Ibadan in 1982, but it wasn't discussed. Who knows, maybe some of the people present were involved in the production. I have a few more questions for you. The majority of African writers are men; if they do not represent or recreate women's experiences faithfully and correctly, then do you feel our responsibility is to correct this by speaking for ourselves?

Asenath: Yes, very much so. Nobody else is going to right these wrongs, just as in the case of colonialism. As Achebe has said, *we* have to right the record. That can be applied to the women question as well. More women writers should come out and give us the dignity we deserve as women and mothers of this continent. The time has come when we should have a networking between those of us who are professors of literature and women writers. We must have a forum where we can work together. We should be able to determine the type of literature our children consume.

Adeola: What is your advice to young girls and even women who wish to become writers?

Asenath: I would just tell them to get up and start writing. If you wish to become a writer, why wait? Get up and write. You may give your writing to somebody who has been publishing to assess it for you; but don't wait.

Adeola: Some people are doing just that. However, both yourself and Flora Nwapa complained that most of the manuscripts you receive are not of a publishable quality.

Asenath: Yes, but I still tell the writers what is wrong and how they can improve. You cannot know whether you can write or not until you have tried. You have to sit down and give yourself a chance, then whoever you send it to will tell you what they think. If it is so bad that it is rejected, what can you do? I think you can read. Read a good book, see how someone else has written and how they go about it and learn it. They say you can teach the technique of writing, but you can't teach writing. You learn from engaging in the act itself.

Adeola: Do you know of an association of African women writers?

Asenath: No, I don't. There used to be an Association of Kenya Writers and I was the Secretary. But since Ngugi went into exile nothing much has been happening. Now I am thinking of calling a meeting so that other people can take over the offices and see what they can do with the association.

Adeola: Of what benefit would the existence of an African women writers' association be?

Asenath: We would have a forum for meeting and comparing notes and learning from one another's experiences. I think we should try and organize it. We have more or less the same problems and we might be able to help one another.

Note

1. Asenath Bole Odaga: 'Popular Literature in East Africa', research paper.

Ifeoma Okoye

Ifeoma Okoye was born in eastern Nigeria. She received her education in Nigeria and is a teacher by profession. Like Pamela Kola, she runs a nursery school in Enugu. Hence, her primary interest is in children's literature, of which she has published many titles such as *Village Boy* (1980), *No School for Eze* (1980), *The Adventures of Tulu the Little Monkey* (1980).

She came to the limelight with the publication of her first novel, *Behind the Clouds* (1982). Her second novel, *Men Without Ears* (1984), won her the Association of Nigerian Authors Award in 1984. In these novels she expresses concern about the moribund direction of Nigerian society, which gives her writing an overt social message.

Work quoted: *Men Without Ears* (UK: Longman, 1984)

14
Ifeoma Okoye

This interview was done by correspondence.

Adeola: *Behind the Clouds* is not a love story in the traditional sense. Have you been able to assess its appeal?

Ifeoma: Yes. I have taught the novel to about 500 students and have also received several letters from people who have read it. From all indications, it is well received, and most people say it is very realistic, though I have been too lenient to Dozie; but all are in sympathy with Ije.

Adeola: Your novels have a class base. Just as Jane Austen dealt with the 18th century English middle class, you write for and about the newly educated class created by the maximisation of educational opportunities after Independence. Why do you consider this group so important?

Ifeoma: Because they are educated, they are the readers in the society. Also because childlessness does not disrupt lower class families as it does middle class, because the former accept polygamy more easily than the latter.

Adeola: Ije is exquisitely drawn. Is she based on someone you know? Do you write from your own life?

Ifeoma: Ije is a purely fictional character. I do not write from my personal situation.

Adeola: The ending of *Behind the Clouds* is optimistic. Can one accuse you of falsifying the truth as it occurs in real life? The Virginias of this world leave too much bitter taste in one's mouth for all to end well in the best of all possible worlds, as you would want us to have it.

Ifeoma: I don't think the ending is too optimistic. In real life things work out well more often than we expect.

Adeola: You are a teacher and you also have a family. How do you fit writing into your life?

Ifeoma: It is not easy. I have many students to teach and marking their work is an ordeal. I also do housework and have an extended family. Because of all these, I write at night.

Adeola: Where does the inspiration to write come from?

Ifeoma: From seeing the injustices, inequality and corruption, around me.

Adeola: The theme of childlessness, and its effect on marriage, which you explore in *Behind the Clouds*, has been explored by Flora Nwapa. Has she influenced you in any way?

Ifeoma: No.

Adeola: What is the future of creativity in Nigeria?

Ifeoma: Not very bright at the moment to put it mildly. There are a lot of problems: not enough encouragement – none at all from the government; publishing houses are contracting, not expanding; books cost fortunes in Nigeria now so only the affluent and committed can afford them. Unfortunately, the affluent are too busy chasing money and the committed are few.

Adeola: As an African woman writer, what barriers have you had to grapple with in order to succeed?

Ifeoma: None.

Adeola: What would be your suggestions to African women who want to write?

Ifeoma: To do just that – write! There's no other way. They will learn from their mistakes. They can also learn by reading other writers and by talking to them.

Adeola: Do you think it will be helpful to have an association of African women writers?

Ifeoma: Yes.

Adeola: You have published two novels and some children's books. When did you know you were a writer?

Ifeoma: When I was first published, in 1980.

Adeola: What is the reaction of your own family to you as a writer?

Ifeoma: They are proud of me and wish me well. As to be expected, one or two are jealous.

Adeola: Your second novel, *Men Without Ears*, is dramatically different in many ways from *Behind The Clouds*, yet they are only two years apart in publication. *Men Without Ears* is a much more ambitious work than the first novel, yet the plot, based mainly on dialogue rather than on narrative, the multiple themes of corruption, moral depravity and absence of values, is deftly handled. It would appear there is a remarkable development in your narrative art within such a short period. Can you explain the genesis of your second novel?

Ifeoma: I wrote this novel while recovering from a major operation. That's the most I can say about its genesis.

Adeola: Another important difference between your first novel and the second is the choice of a male protagonist. Is this deliberate?

Ifeoma: Yes. It suits my themes better.

Adeola: Do you not feel that as one of our very few female African writers you have an obligation to tackle the problems concerning women in our societies first and foremost? The agony that is suffered by a childless woman and the question of infidelity by our men is successfully engaged in *Behind The Clouds*; do you think these two have exhausted the injustices suffered by women in African society?

Ifeoma: My answer to the first part of your question is yes. As for the latter part the answer is no, there are more injustices. Maybe I'll be able to deal with them in future.

Adeola: It is often said that our male writers, with the exception of a few, cannot present believable female characters. How did you find it, creating Chigo, Uloko and their father, all of whom are memorable characters, in their different roles?

Ifeoma: It was not difficult for me. In fact, *Men Without Ears* was one of the easiest of my books to write.

Adeola: One comes across some very strong home truths as one reads *Men Without Ears*. I will cite just two examples of Chigo's numerous observations:

> I was soon to realise . . . that in my country efficiency, scholarship and creativity were not acclaimed. I discovered too that god–fatherism and palm-greasing were better credentials than sound professional qualifications and experience. No wonder mediocrity reigned supreme everywhere. (p. 90).

> After only a few weeks back in Nigeria, I had noticed that what was uppermost in most people's minds, literate and illiterate alike, was making money. I had also noticed that here it was not the man of character who was the greatest of men, but the man of means. (p. 75).

What have been people's reactions to this novel? Have you been satisfied with its reception?

Ifeoma: The novel was declared the best fiction of the year in 1984 by the Association of Nigerian Authors. It has also been translated into Russian. I am, therefore, satisfied with its reception.

Adeola: Are there any idealists like Chigo left in our country? The fate of Chigo remains deliberately ambiguous. He has lost his job and we are left to guess what happens to him next. You seem to be saying that, nevertheless, it remains the supreme responsibility of the artist to present us with possibilities that may be aspired to, and might even be attained, if not in our generation, in the next.

Ifeoma: There are still some idealists in Nigeria but they are very few. People with a strong moral sense survive, but some die for the cause they believe in.

Adeola: What writers have impressed you?

Ifeoma: Pearl S. Buck, Jane Austen, Buchi Emecheta, Daphne du Maurier, Festus Iyayi and Chinua Achebe are some of the authors who have impressed me.

Adeola: Finally, can you briefly describe your creative process? What are your future plans? Do you have any new novels in the pipeline?

Ifeoma: I don't have only one creative process. My novel for young adults, *Chimere*, will be published this year by Longman (Nigeria) Limited in their Gong Series.

'Zulu Sofola

'Zulu Sofola was born in Bendel State, Nigeria, in 1938. She received her primary and secondary education in Nigeria, and then took a B.A. in English from Virginia Union University in the U.S., an M.A. in drama from Catholic University, Washington, D.C., and finally a Ph.D. from the University of Ibadan, Nigeria. She is an accomplished musician, dramatist and director. She joins the critical debate on whether the African writer should write in the local or a foreign language. She has made some incisive statements which have livened up that debate. She is presently professor and head of the Department of Performing Arts at the University of Ilorin, Nigeria. Her plays include *Wedlock of the Gods, Wizard of Law, King Emene, The Sweet Trap, Old Wines Are Tasty, Disturbed Peace of Christmas, Fantasies in the Moonlight, Song of a Maiden,* and *The Operators.* The themes of these plays are wide-ranging, extending from social and domestic comedy to historical tragedy. Her works have been widely performed in Nigeria and have been well known to television viewers since the early seventies.

Work quoted: *King Emene* (U.K., Heinemann: 1974)

15

'Zulu Sofola

This interview was conducted in Ilorin, 7 August 1986.

Adeola: In spite of more than two decades of Independence we Africans are still very much a people without direction, not taken account of and, in fact, despised. To what extend do these realities affect your work?

'Zulu: You will find that most of my writing questions the 'isms' that have been superimposed on African people. Previously, the society was able to fight problems that concerned the society as human beings should do. Now it doesn't seem as if we have a sense of direction or the ability to look inwards to gain insight for solving our problems.

Adeola: What impulse is responsible for your writing? What in your own life, and your background is responsible for your becoming a writer?

'Zulu: I was always questioning something. Then my father was an educationist and he was always telling us about our roots, making us understand what the family lineage had been. But I think mainly it is because I had this inquisitive, questioning mind.

Adeola: In a previous interview (Lee Nichols, 1974) you said your being away from home 'ignited the kind of interest' that pushed you into writing[1]. From your own experience then how would you react to the proposition that writers are born, not made?

'Zulu: I think that writers are born, not made, in terms of the talent it takes to be a writer. However, you do not have to be creative through the writing medium alone, you can be creative as an inventor in whatever area. But the talent has to be there. It is the talent that has to be trained. You cannot put in somebody what she hasn't got. So that statement is true.

Adeola: Are you satisfied with the amount of literary creativity in Nigeria?

'Zulu: I feel that Nigeria is active, very active. But I think it is the kind of writing that is to be questioned. People are asking about commitment and focus and lack of ideology. So if you don't have enough stamina to resist all these, you may find that you are writing propaganda.

Adeola: Why do you think we have so few female writers in Nigeria? (I notice also that even the few are mainly from one ethnic group.) It is a question that was asked recently at an International Black Women Writers' Conference in Michigan. To my mind there was no satisfactory answer to it. Yet I feel the question is significant, and if we answer it truthfully, it might trigger more creativity.

'Zulu: I would like to say that, whatever a woman achieves in her discipline or profession, she achieves it against plenty of odds because a woman's life is more burdened and more confused. Unless the woman is disciplined, thoroughly disciplined, by the end of the day she can't think. She is a burden-carrier, she has to carry herself, she has to carry children, she has to carry a job. She must behave as a wife to her husband, and she has to monitor everything in the house. By the time she goes through a day, and projects for the day after – because unless you plan, at least, four days ahead, you will be stuck – all her time is used up. Then of course for the married professional woman, or even if not married but child-bearing, the period of pregnancy is enough to hold everything back. So that the woman who finally pulls through is virtually ten men in one. It is not as if the women are not ready to do anything, but those who are ready and are willing will have to have some kind of supernatural power!

Adeola: Are there other barriers, inward or outward, that you face in attempting to be a writer?

'Zulu: I don't have any other barriers. As far as I am concerned, I know I have the talent to follow my line of interest, which is writing. I do not follow the wind, by that I mean, I don't allow myself to write what people would like to read. So that I do not have complexes. I do not get terribly attached to my writing. Once I finish a work, and I am satisfied that I have done my best with it then I leave it to find its way, to swim or perish. Whereas some people cling on to what they have written, doing everything to save it against attack. Once they are attuned that way, they find it difficult to take another step. I don't have such complexes, they don't bother me.

Adeola: You are a university teacher, playwright, director, musician, mother and wife. Can you say what is the source of such creative diversity?

'Zulu: The source? (Laughs heartily) Well, I don't know. I don't know. As I might have told you, music was my original interest. But when I was studying in the United States, I had to select another subject in addition to my main line. That was what landed me in drama. But I found that in drama I was also in music because I could produce plays with a musical background and I could use music for the mood. So it was through music that I got into writing.

Adeola: Do you notice any differences in the ways African writers handle theme, character and situations?

'Zulu: Well, yes. Somehow, there is this problem which the educated African – male or female – has, as regards himself. With European exposure the African educated person has been led to believe that the female is an after-thought, a wall–flower, and the man is heaven–sent, the controller of everything. When you look in our literature you find this is how women are portrayed. Even where it is a woman in her own right within the traditional setting, she is going to be portrayed half-way her strength. For example, take *Death and The King's Horseman* by Wole Soyinka (UK: Methuen, 1975). Iyaloja was the head of her hemisphere, she was in charge of the market. But the way in which Soyinka handles the situation the Praise Singer and the Horseman (*Eleshin Oba*) sort of gained dominance over her. You will find that in the hands of female writers as well. It it because we are looking at life this way. Even in Efua Sutherland's *Edufa* (UK: Longman, 1965) you find Aponma surrendering her life for that of a husband who has sold his own soul for wealth. One could understand perhaps that Aponma would behave that way because she was approached through the European image of the woman. But this was in the traditional context, so when her husband confessed to her that her approaching death was the result of a pact which was established over her life, why didn't she run to her people?

Adeola: I wondered whether that was how it was traditionally.

'Zulu: No, no woman within the traditional context would die for a husband. And in fact, they wouldn't want to die for their child either. If the child is the type that is going to take her life, she will make sure that that child does not take her life. Even though it is through you that the child has come to the world, that child's head is different from yours and his destiny is different from yours.

Adeola: What are the questions at the centre of your creative works?

'Zulu: I am motivated by human problems that confront us all. It depends on the spirit of a problem before I get the kind of inspiration which makes me want to write about it. Then I do my research.

Adeola: How have your creative interests evolved? In the earlier interview with Lee Nichols you said you wrote profusely because, 'I found that the more I looked around in the society the more I found so much material that should be utilized'. You wrote eight plays within a very short period, then the pace slackened. Why was that?

'Zulu: It is only that I have been experimenting with different media.

145

For example, there was a period when it looked as if I was hibernating. But I was actually doing a series of plays for television. At the time when that interview took place I hadn't written *Song of A Maiden*, or *The Love of Life* which was commissioned by the World Council of Churches. Three other plays have been commissioned by various other agencies, some of which have not been produced yet. But the pace has not relaxed.

Adeola: Can you describe your creative process? Earlier on, you said you write plays because the process of writing plays suits your temperament: 'When I start I want to go on and I want what I have to say to come right out'. Do you still maintain this position or was that only a phase in your creative career?

'Zulu: It is still on. I was saying that in relation to writing a novel or poetry. You know in the novel form you have to sustain a certain mood for a rather lengthy period. That doesn't happen with plays. In my creative involvement I like to wrap up the action, build the impact, let the characters act themselves out, localize them and then they must go. I don't stop them at a point where I do something else and then go back to them. That is one area of aesthetics where it appears my colleagues do not agree with me, or don't seem to understand me. That is the fact that a character emerges, it is not the writer emerging and fitting herself/himself into the character. That not only includes the character's ethics, view point, it also means language, behaviour and total response to life. If I do not believe in so and so, it doesn't matter, if the character believes in it. You can question the tenets of the character but it isn't necessarily yourself that you are recreating.

Adeola: How do you achieve that?

'Zulu: I am research-oriented in my writing. I don't allow myself artist's liberties, I am always reproducing, as it were, from life.

Adeola: Your *Queen Omu*, which is about the Nigerian Civil War of 1967–70 is a celebration of courageous women. We see woman as nurse, priestess, mother, covered in the blood of childbirth, drawing attention to the unnecessary bloodshed of the foolish fratricidal war or woman as goddess of the river actively protecting her children. Each of these roles is absolutely believable. How did you manage to achieve this?

'Zulu: You know Omu is a priestess. Some of the women you saw in the play were priestessess, some were military people, some were heads of their various institutions. Queen Omu, being the head of the women's arm of the government, was on a par with the king who was the head of the government. So that when the king ran away during the Civil War, automatically, she stepped in. I had to do the research.

Apart from that, my own paternal grandmother was the last Omu before the one in the play, and I saw her place. Her influence is still around. I was able to see it on various levels and I followed this up with my research. Some of the war lyrics too were from my research.

Adeola: The oral traditions play a significant role in your writing. How widespread are the beliefs, practices and ceremonies that control the action in all your plays? For example, the Peace Week, the New Year Festival, the river goddesses and the myth of Lightning and Thunder. How powerful are they in today's society?

'Zulu: They are powerful; they are. The Peace Week is observed every year and within that period everything has to be checked. The Omu has to check the purity of the state and of the stool before they can enter into the Peace Week. Now, however, the strictness in terms of the king staying within an enclosure during that whole period has been relatively relaxed. He stays in an inner parlour where he can receive a few people, then he goes right back. The day he comes out is the day of the New Year Festival.

In *Old Wines Are Tasty*, the hero did not get the support of the people because of his attitude to tradition, and that practice is still there. He was rendered incapable of governing because of his disrespect for tradition. Many people are now beginning to realize that without the traditional base they just don't have any voice at all. Igbo society is strict, it is not as relaxed as Yoruba society.

Adeola: The language of the oral tradition permeates your work. In *King Emene*, Ojei speaking to the King says:

> The earth says that a corpse is not a new thing to her. Problems are nothing new to mankind but the truth remains that while some are frightened by their problems others allow their problems to crush them; still there are others who rather than allow their problems to frighten or crush them, would face them squarely and conquer them. (p. 32)

How do you manage to capture the tone and content of traditional speech-pattern in your plays?

'Zulu: I listen. I listen and I do not go about feeling that people are inferior because that is how they express themselves. I wouldn't fit this man within the speech-style of a university professor, because he belongs to royalty. He will talk within his context in terms of imagery and philosophy and it will fit the style. This style is most visible in *The Song of A Maiden* where you have the professors 'doing their own thing' at a Senate meeting. Then we go to the Oba's council and it is a different language that is spoken. But both are on an equal level. The only way to achieve a realistic rendering is by listening.

Adeola: In all your plays except in *Queen Omu-Ako of Oligbo*, women are in the background. In that play, the women seemed to have understood better than the men, that the Civil War was pointless, and that whether it was Federal or Biafran soldiers that were killed, they were all human beings. Would you say that this deliberate focus on the feminine role in the Civil War marks a new direction in your creativity?

'Zulu: Well, no. I think this play just happens to be completely on women. In *King Emene*, the Omu was there and she was the one who told the King, frankly and fearlessly, that he was the cause of the problem. That was her role in that play. Even though critics feel I was deliberately making a woman stronger, that was how she would have acted in real life. I have seen this very Omu-Ako confront the King at a festival.

In *The Sweet Trap* we have another type of story. There I was handling women who were affected by the European super-imposition; women who did not know who they were and where they were going. They were absolutely irrelevant and they were fighting the kind of fight that was almost like the chasing of a shadow. Then they distrupted the society. In that play women are seen in a different context, the European-oriented context.

In *Old Wines are Tasty* I have the mother who would find herself in a big dilemma because the institution that made her free to have children for a lover also made it possible for her husband to reject those children when he got his own natural sons. She was urged to have a lover to provide a son for her husband. She obeyed and followed the tradition, but later paid for her obedience. The society was very unfair to her but it wasn't a fight that she could fight alone, as Ogboma did in *The Wedlock of the Gods* where she defied everybody.

Adeola: But look what happened to her!

'Zulu: Look what happened to her indeed! Nevertheless, I feel that one should do whatever one is committed to do. But once you disturb whatever is there, the repercussions will crush you, unless you have the strength to resist.

Adeola: Yes, this is what happens in Ama Ata Aidoo's *Anowa*.

'Zulu: Yes, that is true. So if you say 'I believe I can marry whoever I want' and disrupt things that will affect even the unborn, how can you avoid the repercussions of your deliberate action?

Adeola: On whose side are you then? You seem to be saying that if one feels this commitment to modernization, one should act according to one's vision but one should be prepared to face the consequences because one will be disturbing age-old traditions.

'Zulu: No, no, these are not age-old traditions. You will be disturbing the moral pattern of the society. For instance, in Ogboma's case, by the time the play ends three violent deaths have occurred, either by homicide or suicide. Those violent deaths are going to affect the families because of re-incarnation. You understand me? That is the reason why the people do not approve of violent death.

Since Ogboma and Uloko have decided they are going to get together come what may, they have disturbed the moral strength of the society. Ogboma is supposed to be in mourning for her husband's death, yet she is entertaining a lover to the point where she gets pregnant. Now, that adultery has implications because it disturbs the normal psychological pain of death and mourning. It disturbs the moral health of the society and brings suffering to many. That is not good for anybody.

Adeola: I agree with you, but my strong misgiving stems from the fact that the original marriage was forced upon Ogboma.

'Zulu: Yes, the marriage was not a healthy one. The girl's father was wrong and therefore he should also accept the consequences. He has lost a daughter and three people have died. But you cannot say that because the girl was in love, it justified the tragedy that followed. Her actions precipitated something which, once in motion, could not be stopped. So it means you cannot reach a certain point and then try to turn back. Uloko had the courage to fight because he believed that his destiny was to be her husband. According to the people's belief-system, if you are convinced, then you should fight, even if it requires your life. The couple were caught in a web, because the girl felt the brother-in-law would have raped her if she had waited.

Adeola: If you are interested in tackling the woman's experience in our society there is no shortage of themes. For example, we are aware of the ineffectuality of the Osu laws and the law limiting the amount of dowry that can be required because both traditional systems have led to negative experiences, particularly for women.

On a broader scale, Toni Bambara feels that 'the anger, dismay, disappointment, or just sheer bewilderment that many women experience as a way of life in regard to the man-woman set up is something we're all going to have to get used to airing'.[2] To me the need for this is far more urgent now than ever before. How do you react to this?

'Zulu: As for the Osu system, that will have to wipe itself out gradually. There is no way you can legislate for it. Even in the advanced countries where they have legislation with regard to minority groups, people have found ways of evading it. The Osu system is especially serious because the Osu are descendants of people sacrificed alive, and in the belief system, human beings should not deprive the god of what has been given to him. Christianity came and presented the Osu as outcasts; they were really meant to be sacred.

As for dowry, the whole thing has been mishandled and miscontrued. Where it has now become a big problem is where fathers see their daughters as a means of money-making, a kind of investment, which was not how it used to be. The bride money was very small, something like 40 naira. The rest of the money was spent to buy all that the bride would require to start a new life in her husband's house. This system was established by the people, in every part of Nigeria, to make sure that the woman had enough to live on, in case the husband decided to take a new wife. If the woman is brought into the house without this type of preparation, the man could fill up his house with wives without any provision for them. Every woman is supposed to have a way of maintaining and sustaining herself in a polygamous system. She shouldn't depend on the husband. A man who brings in a wife without going through what is required to make him a man, is going to treat that wife as though she has no value. I am not in agreement with those who say they want to go to their husband's house without the man fulfilling all that is required by the traditions. The dowry is the contract, and the bride money is symbolic, like the ring. If the women who are talking this way looked into the truth of the institution, they would start insisting on their rights and put their fathers where they belong. For example, if the father has taken 4,000 naira from the husband, the wife should demand it and put it to her own use, or take various things to the value of what her husband paid.

Adeola: Can African women writers help to resolve some of the debates concerning our underdevelopment and the oppression of women by men?

'Zulu: I have always said that the only way that the African woman of today, with her European orientation which we call education, can be liberated, is to study the traditional system and the place of the woman as defined by it. There was no area of human endeavour in the traditional system where the woman did not have a role to play. She was very strong and very active. The only woman who has made history within the European structure was Mrs Funmilayo Ransome-Kuti, but even she used the traditional system[3]. Take the historical heroines – Moremi, Idhia, Queen Amina, even this Omu who we have just talked about; they achieved whatever they did through their traditional role or office[4]. In the European system there is absolutely no place for the woman. In the traditional system the roles are clearly demarcated. For example, recently someone was telling me that a woman can never be an *Oba* (a traditional chief). So I replied that that was true; but the other side of the coin is that the *Oba* can never be *Iyalode* (traditional head of women's affairs). The *Obi* can never be an *Omu*. The two positions exist, one cannot usurp the role of the other. The thing is that in the traditional system the human being was recognized as a human being.

Adeola: Female writers are in the minority in Africa. Do you consider them a significant force in African literature? Can we talk about a feminine literary tradition?

'Zulu: I think we can talk about female writers but I am not sure that we have evolved any feminine literary tradition as yet. Each woman writer is handling the problem as she sees it, she is not taking a special female outlook as such. But it may boil down to that after a while because the woman is going to see a woman's role more clearly if she examines our tradition.

Adeola: Would a union of African women writers give greater weight to the collective voice of women in Africa?

'Zulu: I don't think so. What we need is proper writing, which people will read and accept. But if you want to struggle in a particular area, it would be better done in other ways than through writing.

Adeola: Many women writers have complained about the problem of publishing.

'Zulu: That is because they do not hustle like men. I feel it might help if women could come together and work through feminist publishing houses.

Adeola: Tell me something about the reception of your plays in Nigeria. Do you think you have been accorded the recognition you deserve?

'Zulu: Well, I think so. I don't know. However, I don't believe in setting myself a target for satisfaction. As I said earlier, when I finish writing, that is it. As long as I convince myself that I have done my best, that if the work were returned to me to re-do, I couldn't improve on it any way, then at that stage I am through with it. But I don't expect people to treat me in a special way.

Adeola: To go back to the actual plays, all your heroes and heroines are people who commit something abominable, who are in conflict with tradition. What is responsible for this? Who needs to change – the society or the people? On whose side are you? Do you feel that there are any aspects of our tradition that need changing?

'Zulu: It seems as if people think that the way you portray the society in your play and manipulate certain characters to win, is how you wish it to be in real life. In *Wedlock of the Gods*, which is about a forbidden union between a widow and her chosen lover, the couple decided to resist society and society choked them. This should make the audience uncomfortable and encourage them to see that something is done to change it. How else are you going to bring about a change if you don't make people see the consequences of their actions? You cannot make them feel that the problems are solved, because they are not. People have to be prepared to fight and change our society.

Adeola: *Song of a Maiden* is a powerful play exposing the bankruptcy of Nigerian academics. Seen against the back-cloth of the solid tradition which they have spurned, they look puny and riduculous. As you yourself are a member of the educated elite, it seems you have lashed out strongly against members of your class. How have they received the play?

'**Zulu**: They are not happy, but so it is. You call yourself a professor and all you do is pour out jargon from a book, whilst all the problems are left unsolved. I am an academic too, but the fact is that we are all useless.

Adeola: The river goddess appears in *Queen Omu* as well as in *Song of a Maiden*. You seem to have special interest in her. In both instances she is a protector of her children. Do people really believe in her?

'**Zulu**: During the Civil War, they said that the river goddess was at the war front. When the war was over they said she came back and they saw her foot-prints marked in white chalk on the road. That is a reality. The river goddess who was seen at Agbor and the one at Asaba about whose coming the prophet had pronounced years past are also historical facts.

Adeola: How would you comment on the statement that writing is keeping track of one's own being?

'**Zulu**: I would like to extend it to 'keeping track of one's own being as a part of the entire human race', for what happens to me affects others. According to Donne the death of one man diminishes me. That is how I see it.

Adeola: Which of your characters is closest to your own heart?

'**Zulu**: I think, the tragic hero in *Old Wines Are Tasty*. He came pure-hearted, he didn't know the truth about his parentage. By the time he knew what was happening, he couldn't go back to Lagos. He is unlike the others, who were partly responsible for their own tragedy, like Ogboma, who defied society. In both cases the society is harsh on women. These are the areas the 'women's lib' groups should look into, particularly the position of a woman who becomes a widow. Whether we work or do not work, whether we have the vote or not, these are the problems that came with westernization, they are not genuine problems.

Adeola: How do we determine which ones are genuine African problems arising from our tradition?

'**Zulu**: If we look closely we will discover what our real problems are. For example, because a man has not succeeded in having a son, he decides his daughter should bear the son for him. Meanwhile, his new wife has his child, and the daughter is now free to go and get married, but the husband that is marrying her cannot marry her and the child. These are some anomalies in the tradition which shouldn't be.

Adeola: A Nigerian critic has observed that there are few African women playwrights. She speculates the reason could be 'that being a play-writer implied production, working in a theatre, . . . at all hours, in the company of men. Such a profession would be a source of insecurity for some husbands'.[5]

Could you comment on these speculations both from the point of view of a dramatist and a producer?

'**Zulu**: That is true. The playwright has to spend a lot of time outside the home. A woman producer has problems both with the male and female characters and has to have iron stamina to deal with them. Husbands present their own problem. If you tell your husband that you are going to the theatre, and you get there and you find you have to use another venue, you must leave word there that if your husband happens to come looking for you, to direct him to where you are. After he has done it a few times he will understand and he will have faith in you. A man in your place will not show that type of concern. A woman has to put in all the effort to keep her profession as well as her home. Without this careful management, the husband might decide one day to go and get another wife because, after all he is an African. It is still all right because if you look at it from the traditional point of view as my mother puts it: 'You didn't circumcize him and you cannot put his thing in your handbag, so how can you tell him where to go?'

Adeola: On this note of generosity and acceptance let me ask the last question. What is your concept of commitment as a writer? Do you agree with Ogundipe–Leslie who says: 'The female African writer should be committed in three ways: as a writer as a woman and a Third World person; and her womanhood is implicated in all three'?

'Zulu: That is what you have to be, there is no other way.

Notes

1. Interview with Lee Nichols, *Conversations*, Voice of American Publications, 1974.
2. Toni Cade Bamabara: Interview in G. Hull (ed), *Black Women Writers at Work* (US: Oldcastle, 1984).
3. A women's leader and political activist in the 1930's in Abeokuta, south-west Nigeria.
4. Moremi is a legendary heroine of the Yoruba people of south-west Nigeria, who saved the historic town of Ile-Ife from marauders. Idhia was a Bini heroine, a member of the royal house of Benin. Queen Amina was ruler of the northern Nigerian kingdom of Zaria in the 16th. century.
5. Molara Ogundipe–Leslie: 'The Female Writer and Her Commitment,' in *Women in African Literature Today*, No. 15, eds. Eldred Durosimi Jones, Eustace Palmer and Marjorie Jones (UK: James Currey, 1987), p. 10.

Acknowledgements

The research leading to the writing of this book was undertaken during my sabbatical leave from the University of Guyana in 1985–86. I am grateful to my university for allowing me time off to do this research, and also wish to express my appreciation to the Commonwealth Secretariat for the travel grant which enabled me to travel in Africa to collect the necessary data.

A great debt is owed to many friends and relations in Africa who assisted me in the work: the Sawyers in Ghana; Professor and Mrs. Okoth-Ogendo in Kenya; Horace and Makini Campbell in Dar-es-Salaam; Professor Bolanle Awe and Dr. Mosun Omibiyi-Obidike of the University of Ibadan, Nigeria.

Finally, I acknowledge my indebtedness to all the writers who warmly received me and cooperated with me; to my family who learnt to do without me; and to Mrs. Bibi Khan, University of Guyana, Department of English Secretary, for typing the manuscript.